A World Without Racism

A World Without Racism

Building Antiracist Futures

Edited by Joshua Virasami

First published 2024 by Pluto Press
New Wing, Somerset House, Strand, London WC2R 1LA
and Pluto Press, Inc.
1930 Village Center Circle, 3-834, Las Vegas, NV 89134

www.plutobooks.com

British Library Cataloguing in Publication Data
A catalogue record for this book is available from the British Library

ISBN   978 0 7453 4809 4   Paperback
ISBN   978 0 7453 4811 7   PDF
ISBN   978 0 7453 4810 0   EPUB

This book is printed on paper suitable for recycling and made from
fully managed and sustained forest sources. Logging, pulping and
manufacturing processes are expected to conform to the environmental
standards of the country of origin.

Typeset by Stanford DTP Services, Northampton, England

Simultaneously printed in the United Kingdom and United States of
America

Contents

Introduction:
A World Without Racism

Joshua Virasami

A few months ago, Marion, a resident in Hackney where one of our local tenant union branches organises, called me up, desperately explaining her housing issues. Marion had been forced into costly temporary accommodation,[1] prohibited from having visits and unable to move her sick mother from the top floor due to faulty lifts, and was sharing facilities communally with dozens of other families. 'A prisoner' is how she described her experience. Tens of thousands of recently arrived migrants to Britain are routinely placed in temporary accommodation, in rooms sometimes separated by sheets, and given food so inadequate that mothers are malnourished and unable to breastfeed, where roofs fall in on playing children and regular outbreaks of diseases plunge hundreds into ill health. On occasion, these inhumane facilities are placed under strict curfew because of arson attacks by racist vigilante mobs.[2] A few weeks later, when running a training session with members, using the Haitian Revolution as a case study for self-organised political struggle, a member from our West London Branch, again a Black migrant woman, told the group: 'We're still slaves, just different masters.' To many immigrants navigating life on this small post-imperial island, a racially inflected, authoritarian nationalism carries with it almost all the registers of the slave-owning time gone by. In Britain, where both the Labour and Conservative parties trade on unanimous adoptions of nostalgic nationalist resentment, where it's always 'British this for British that', rebuilding a revitalised antiracism, one which can form the basis of a unified, internationalist working class, is a matter of life or death.

This collection consists of ten chapters written by ten different groups at the forefront of antiracist organising in Britain. Within this book you will encounter activists resisting immigration regimes, waging a new era of feminist struggle, reimagining healing and health, resisting the expansion of the police state, organising for access to food and land, fighting British imperialism through internationalism and fighting for climate justice, for a just and emancipatory education system, for empowering cultural expression and for safe, secure and dignified housing. If race, as Stuart Hall wrote, is the modality through which class is lived, then these ten chapters address the struggles through which class is felt and rebuked. Fighting racism today means fighting it at every corner. If we are to deal with the historic specificity of race and racism, to theorise racial capitalism in this moment, we need to be in conversation with those currently undertaking active political struggle among the racialised poor and the broader working class.

As a collection, this book has three primary motivations:

1. Creating an archive of this moment of antiracist resistance from below, one that can facilitate ongoing learning in times to come. Similar projects, such as when members of the Brixton Black Women's Group got together to write 'Heart of the Race' in 1985, have played a critical role in helping ensure lessons are not lost but endure and help us decipher the origins of the present crisis we find ourselves in, and a way out.

2. Further our understanding of the ways in which our struggles meet and speak to one another, where our strategies, demands, principles and opponents might align enough that we can say they may be confidently adopted across movements. This might be understood as the practice of popularising our struggles: a proactive rather than reactive approach. As activist and educator Aviah Day describes, 'we need to look at ways to *cause* conflict'.[3]

3. Helping us take a big step forwards in building a broad-based antiracist, feminist, anti-capitalist historical bloc capable of mobilising millions in an effective counter-attack to the forms of mass dispossession and domination we're experiencing.

Ultimately, I hope this book allows antiracist activists to effectively think through the present and transform it.

I encourage you to interrogate the following questions while reading this book. How does the antiracist organising laid out here help us understand how we can build a broader alliance of forces and popular demands? How can antiracist organising be a truly unified, multicultural force for change? How do we build stronger circuits of solidarity across the national and global level?

These ten chapters represent what we might call antiracism from below, which is part of centuries-old emancipatory traditions, an antiracism charged with militant feminism, with internationalism and with a searing critique of racial capitalism. Today, however, antiracism from above is ubiquitous. Antiracism from above, already well scaffolded by the 1980s, is the organised counterattack by the capitalist class in response to militant, antiracist trade union organising, mass mobilisations, Black Power organisations, insurgent literature and more. Ilyas Nagdee and Azfar Shafi's recent book, *Race to the Bottom*, documents the process through which grassroots antiracism is worn down through a three-pronged political strategy of corporatism, representation and civic power, which is often state-funded and proliferates throughout racialised communities. The shift from black power to civic power is prolific, everywhere one looks there is an absence of the kinds of independent, militant community-led resistance – organisations like the Newham Monitoring Project – and an abundance of third sector organisations doing remedial work within a fundamentally different, often liberal, paradigm; seeking redress through the system, as opposed to presenting a direct challenge to the legitimacy of the systems as they exist. The availability of state funding for this kind of community work was not accidental, but as chronicled by Nagdee and Shafi, one of many intentional strategies to defang antiracism.

Across the 1970s and 1980s in Britain the Race Today Collective, a lodestar of antiracism from below, provided both rigorous journalism and analysis via their journal *Race Today*,[4] while militants such as Farrukh Dondy, Barbara Beese, Jean Ambrose, Mala Sen, Leila Hassan-Howe and Darcus Howe helped coordinate powerful moments of resistance, such as the Black People's Day of Action. But why the name *Race Today*? I like to think of it as an ode to the need to understand antiracism as a constant inquiry into the contemporary conjuncture they faced: an effort to highlight the residual colonial racisms, unpack the newly hegemonic neoliberal reordeing, and in the face of it assert an insurgent antiracist anticapitalism against the ruling class. Race, racism and capitalism are never a closed book, and '[c]atching history on the wing', as Ambalavaner Sivanandan put it, requires us to analyse the ever-shifting terrain beneath us and then leap from it.

Being an antiracist today means grappling with the shadow of defeat; taking a balance sheet of our losses not just to antiracism from above but to the rise of Thatcherism within which the counterattack was couched. If, as Arun Kundnani argues, 'the past cannot serve as an alibi for the present',[5] then the present is where we are left: where we are set the task of thinking through the conjuncture we are in.

Thinking with the present and thinking with agents of emancipatory traditions, as Michael Denning writes, is a longstanding progressive tradition. It means recognising that waging struggle today requires taking stock of how struggle was waged up to this moment, what worked and what failed, what dangers and what opportunities lie before us, what the origins of the crisis we're facing are, what insurgent ideas and forces are emerging and therefore what alliance of forces – political, cultural, social, intellectual – might see us through to a moment of socio-political renewal. Antonio Gramsci, considered by many to be a master of thinking through political defeat and opportunity, foregrounded the need for producing questions of the very things we often take for granted, maintaining that we cannot be deterministic about the present, as it neither arrives to us as inevitable nor as the outcome of simply the economic, political, social or cultural.

Thinking Through …

This collection champions the voices of antiracists who are embattled at a time when there is a war for the soul of antiracism, and no clear winner yet. Nearly every mainstream tabloid, news broadcaster and Conservative Party front bencher has lined up to remind the public that people like those in this book are not 'wholesome antiracists' but opportunists who are using race to advance a dangerous agenda. It's worth asking, what makes an antiracist 'wholesome' and what makes them a dangerous or 'controversial' antiracist? Such designations have attached to me by many news outlets since I began doing activism. Satnam Virdee provocatively charted the role of 'racialised outsiders' in the making of the English working class,[6] and perhaps it's also now prudent to recognise, as Jonas Marvin writes, that there are also racialised *insiders*,[7] who are not just tolerant of but emboldening a version of antiracism championed by the political and corporate establishment. In a situation like this, some antiracists will be lauded, awarded, sponsored and promoted, while some of us will be vilified, harassed, investigated and threatened.

A world without racism, an uncontroversial demand, can quickly become a threatening declaration when made by the *wrong* person, that is, when it is charged with *real* anti-establishment politics because, as current Secretary of State Kemi Badenoch argues, we are not well-meaning activists but instead a real 'political movement' – an intolerable threat to business as usual – and the establishment is working around the clock to prevent its re-emergence. To Badenoch, Prime Minister Rishi Sunak and Home Secretary James Cleverly, antiracist struggles are a reminder of the unresolved contradictions of neoliberalism, primarily its inability to universalise the promise of equality and democracy. In this context, race provides the perfect alibi; for the ruling class it's not that racialised populations were never *actually* guaranteed equality, rather it is down to our own shortcomings. We're told that our communities do not possess enough gusto, enough individualism (or conversely too much communalism) or enough entrepreneurial spirit, or worse, our foreign cultures are hampering us, our family are structures inadequate or we indulge in victim narratives.[8] All of these accusations are aimed at bringing race and racism back to the comfortable terrain of clashing cultures, neatly tucked away from the need to overhaul global oppressive systems.

There are powerful actors in British society who want to ensure that books like this one simply don't exist. When we secured funding to enable the authors of this collection to resource their research and writing we soon found ourselves under attack from a team of journalists, lawyers and regulatory bodies in tow, publishing hit pieces and deploying their resources against myself and our funder (who temporarily shut down their entire operations), effectively driving a wedge between us and sparking a month-long battle for the financial survival of the project. It is not an overstatement to say that these actors – the media barons, corporate class and politicians – are intent on ensuring our antiracism from below does not root itself as a popular form of politics.

*　*　*

Being a prominent figure in the Black Lives Matter movement in Britain has its dangers: some expected, such as having a *Daily Mail* journalist parked outside my house-share all day in a 4×4 BMW, asking neighbours for a scoop, being hauled to the Old Bailey for riot-related charges or being discussed on far-right forums and targeted by right-wing lawyers. Other instances were unexpected, for example being doxed by other antiracist activists for not being 'Black enough' and having mine and others' racial *authenticity* questioned, notably on the additional basis that we all seemed, or were, Muslim. The activist in question received thousands of likes for said 'call-out'. I also did not expect for the lead musician from a popular hip-hop group (and other prominent cultural figures for that matter) to engage in a pile-on of BLMUK, which was readily lapped up by the *Daily Mail*, because we were, essentially, too anti-capitalist. But these individual instances are only symptoms that point out an intellectual weakness at the heart of antiracism, as it is commonly viewed and interpreted. Race and antiracism are grossly misunderstood. In fact, they arrive from some of our own people as ideology from above; race as an apolitical, neutral, natural taxonomy and antiracism as the need to bolster individualism and entrepreneurial spirit within our communities.

One explanation for this weakness might be that antiracism today is severed from its radical predecessors: the Black Power movements of the 1970s and 1980s. This is no doubt part of the problem. Another equally convincing diagnosis is that we're relying on what's lying around us – theoretically, practically and strategically – when we desperately need to be building refreshed narratives around racism, racial capitalism and imperialism. In lieu of that work, people seeking out how to be an antiracist today are met with a heady cocktail of antiracism(s) fresh off the self-help bookshelf. If antiracism is about allyship with or deference to racialised people, if it is about a seeming hierarchy of racial oppression, if it is about a lack from within racialised communities, and if racism is presented as a pathology of white people, it is simply not fit to restructure society, it is in essence still imbued with the residual and dominant ideologies we need to overcome.

There are no shortcuts to working through our present moment. When Milton Friedman, one of the primary architects of neoliberal capitalism, shrewdly noted that in a crisis people tend to reach for the ideas lying around, he was speaking about the strategic wager of neoliberalism – to plant its economic theory far and wide in preparation for a crisis, so it becomes a useful set of ideas that people reach for when the going gets tough. So, what are *we* reaching for? And most importantly, what are *we* planting?

Many of the authors in this collection take stock of the increasingly authoritarian turn the British state has taken in the last decade, whether through their struggles to kill the new policing bill or to fight the way border enforcement is encroaching on our everyday lives. Indeed, from their vantage point the organising principle of racism today is often found in authoritarian nationalisms, in the weaponisation of cultural differences, in the spectre of the migrant, the Muslim or the Black boy. At a time when the presiding feeling on the streets is dog-eat-dog, Migrants Organise, Sisters Uncut and a number of other contributors speak about the work of building communities of resistance across differences, and how solidarity built through struggle offers the only real antidote to communities riven by division, individualism and resentment. Moreover, through these chapters a picture emerges of a wholesale organised abandonment of the working class, where the plan, as economist Gary Stevenson remarks, is to make everyone permanently poorer. Put differently, our communities are under siege in a period of heightened, racialised class war.

* * *

My cousin, a few good mates and I found ourselves crouched on the grass verges overlooking the car park to the Curry's superstore in Brixton on Sunday 7 August 2011, as a deafening police helicopter sped down above us bending over a nearby tree and knocking one of us over. Two of us rushed down to the open bays as the helicopter slowed, dropped its searchlight directly onto us like some kind of scene from a cartoon, and instructed us to STOP. We didn't stop, and nor could we. The remains of the inside of the superstore, like the scorched cars, burned away any pretences I had regarding the permanence of business as usual.

Of the over 3,000 predominately young people shopped through Keir Starmer's (then director of public prosecutions) controversial 24-hour courts, most were convicted of looting-related crimes. Most of the riots involved people taking things they didn't have or couldn't have. Steven Kavanagh, third in command at the Metropolitan Police at the time (now second in command at INTERPOL), when being interviewed on Radio 4 declared that the riots sweeping across England were examples of organised greed and criminality.[9] Greed is, at its essence, about excess, but since these young people, disproportionately racialised, were three times more likely than the average person to be out of work, the notion of greed as weaponised by the ruling class was certainly working harder than it should to explain the riots.

Brixton, home to big, bustling migrant communities, like count-less urban centres, was in the middle of an attack in slow motion, an attack that today is turning into full-scale war as decades of neolib-eralism's assault is leaving swathes of people out of work, without a home and out of options. Gentrification – the selling off of social housing stock and one of the most rapacious forms of this accumu-lation via expropriation – had been working its way deep under the skin of places such as Brixton, displacing people mercilessly.[10] Of course, side by side with gentrification and acting as the fuse setting off the riots is the violent, sometimes deadly, policing of our com-munities, where we see benefits replaced by batons to further control surplus populations through discipline and punishment.[11]

So, if the riots weren't simply organised greed, then what was hap-pening? Why, in fact, were riots and rebellions a staple feature across the world in the early 2010s and since, even making *TIME* maga-zine's person of the year, *the protestor*? 'People that have got nothing', one 'looter' explained, 'wanted to show they had nothing'.[12] In some ways this quote encapsulates not just the riots taking place in Britain but much of what took place globally. Mohamed Bouazizi, regarded as the trigger to the Tunisian Revolution and the 'Arab Spring', who set himself alight on the streets of Sidi Bouzid in Tunisia eight months prior to the riots in Britain – in a town with an unemploy-ment rate of 30 per cent – showed that, following years of impoverishment and violent contact with the police, *he had nothing.*[13] The dramatic proliferation of this condition for racialised populations all over the world, of being exploited to the point of having nothing, is far more widespread than when Bouazizi died. Today we see how it is still ripping through communities and spread-ing its misery everywhere. Ten years later, what kind of opportunities lie out there for a generation who came of age in the riots? Earlier this year a new report shone light on how underemployment in Britain is becoming a new normal,[14] where working a full eight-hour shift is rare, stringing together shifts and jobs are common and pension contributions have become a thing of the past. This is heightened wage exploitation, zero hours on steroids. The key feature of this condition of working-class life today is captured in the feeling of being 'underutilised', unproductive or simply superfluous to the system. Michael Denning, in an essay on 'wageless life', accurately captured this immiserating reality when noting that 'under capitalism, the only thing worse than being exploited is not being exploited'.[15]

The condition of having nothing was once described as being a pauper. The contradiction is that the promise of capitalism, we're taught, would, similarly to a great global anti-virus, eradicate this bug in the system, turning every human into a free labourer, able to dispense with their labour on the market and earn a wage in a world of entrepreneurship, innovation and seamless mass production. The reality for most of the world's racialised populations, and increasingly for those whose wages might have once been propped up (temporarily) by whiteness, is that capitalism does not provide life, it takes it away, rendering billions as surplus to its promise of prosperity and security.

The dramatic rise of pauperism in the eighteenth and nineteenth centuries, Karl Marx observed, was in fact contingent on the rise of capitalism and the enclosures of common land which preceded it. There is a dialectical relationship between pauperism and private property. Marx was no stranger to pauperism himself, losing four young children to poverty and suffering himself from ailments due to poor housing; acutely aware of what it meant to be a superfluous, stateless Jew, he noted in 1861 that 'it is already contained in the concept of the free labourer, that he is a pauper.' From this he draws a more damning conclusion: 'He can live as a worker only in so far as he exchanges his labour capacity … this exchange is tied to conditions which are accidental *for him*, and indifferent to his *organic* presence. He is thus a virtual pauper.'[16] These words allow us to return to the theme of this section. Neoliberalism is a mask which is slipping to reveal that under capitalism we are born paupers: not humans, not workers. Put differently, to be made disposable under the eyes of capital we must always already be inherently superfluous;[17] we are inherently worthless unless capital breathes life into us.

How do we address head-on this interminable condition of working-class life under capitalism? How do we address racism and capitalism with something visionary? How do we begin our march toward a new kind of human civilisation? The words *collective liberation* surface across the entire collection. To the authors here, only a liberatory vision of a world to win can counter oppression. Fred Hampton, the trailblazing chairman of the Chicago chapter of the Black Panther Party in the 1960s, when speaking to an audience on the liberatory politics of the Black Panthers, provided a similar answer: 'We don't think you fight fire with fire best; we think you fight fire with water best. We're going to fight racism not with racism, but we're going to fight with solidarity. We say we're not going to fight capitalism with black capitalism, but we're going to fight it with socialism.'[18] Solidarity and socialism, Hampton argues, are the political arsenal we can turn to, build with and offer as an alternative to the moral malaise of racial capitalism. What is the vision we are offering to one another and our communities, as a way out of this terrifying conjuncture?

Leaping From …

In the 14 years I've engaged in political activism I've had the honour of engaging with dozens upon dozens of local groups, institutions and national organisations, including most in this book. I've travelled from community halls to campuses, from Cardiff to Glasgow, working with climate groups to trade union delegates and everyone in between. I've spoken to tens of thousands and to a room of five. It is plainly clear to me that the ten groups in this collection are emblematic of something enormous, a multitude of social forces, thousands of groups, all resisting in some way or another the wrath of racial capitalism. This is our power. In these 14 years, the single occasion where the energy, connections and commitment of these social classes were leveraged almost all at once was the rallying around the political force of Jeremy Corbyn. The question then, as it is now, is how do we build an alliance and synergy between the social and political forces, one which is owned by and accountable to the masses within the grassroots: how do we build a confident, broad, counter-hegemonic bloc?

Seeking to transform this moment, as Mohamed Elnaiem explains in Chapter 4, is about making the politically *impossible* the politically *inevitable*. An important starting point in this endeavour is the recognition that capitalism always progresses in fits and starts, that it is a history full of ifs, buts and maybes, and that therefore the preservation of its ruling class has never been and can never be a done deal: the impossible is always possible. It is, in that sense, always a matter of tilting the odds evermore in our own favour, building the right alliance of forces and leveraging them effectively. Making the impossible possible was a longstanding interest of the late Chilean educator and public intellectual Marta Harnecker:

> Politics can also not be limited to the art of what is possible. For the left, politics must be the art of making the impossible possible. This is not some kind of voluntarist statement. What I am talking about is understanding politics as the art of constructing social and political forces that are capable of changing the balance of forces to the benefit of the popular movements, and making possible in the future what today appears to be impossible.[19]

Before coming to the question of an alliance of forces, however, it's important to foreground the question of political principles. The chapters in this collection powerfully extend a number of principles which can guide not just the wider antiracist social movements but also any possible coming together of broader progressive forces. However we leap from this moment, it must be principled, drawing from the distilled wisdom of social movements.

Throughout the chapters in this book there are illustrations of powerful campaigns within working-class communities. These campaigns are the front line of working-class struggle, containing great potential to *cause* conflict – to heighten the contradictions. As Chapter 5 explains, by way of Ambalavaner Sivanandan, our aims should always be to turn 'cases into issues, issues into causes, and causes into a movement'. There are well-established pedagogies of resistance which are instructive in thinking through how to turn causes into movements, not least the form of the 'defence committee' which the Northern Police Monitoring Project writes about in Chapter 2. If we want to join forces across our movements, these working-class, antiracist campaigns are the inroads. Though these campaigns often address a site of injustice, be it the border, the prison or the housing estate, they are indictments of the whole system. Often we see in the chapters how the sites are connected and how there is ample opportunity for cross-fertilisation between different social and political forces. Constructing forces is not an abstract endeavour; the only way to draw together meaningful alliances is through forging common struggles which address head-on the material conditions of the working class.

Constructing forces requires manual as well as intellectual labour, which means we need to be fighting fit. Healing Justice London, writing about their community research project and exhibition, 'death by a thousand cuts', highlight the impact of austerity within their communities. In this they are not alone. A number of authors talk of youth programmes or direct action aimed at addressing the impacts of the ongoing class war fought through the neoliberal austerity agenda. The very services which enable our communities to reproduce themselves, abilities fought for and won through the delivery of social welfare, from mental health provisions to childcare, have been decimated by austerity. In these circumstances, where indebtedness, low wages, poor housing conditions and malnutrition are the hallmarks of everyday life for millions, groups such as No More Exclusions and Land in Our Names allude to the need to 'build life-affirming institutions' in the here and now. Survival pending revolution, Huey P. Newton wrote, was about raising political consciousness while meeting the urgent needs of the community through a number of survival programmes, from their sickle cell research units to the intercommunal youth institute.

The most frightening spectre to the ruling class, and one of the reasons antiracism from below as it existed in the 1970s could not be tolerated by them, was its spirit of internationalism. An internationalist working class in Britain is not a distant memory, as Chapter 4 outlines; it is in many ways a great tradition of emancipatory struggles in Britain. As pro-Palestinian mobilisations in recent months have demonstrated, the working class in Britain are ready in their millions to organise around and talk about the ways in which imperialism must be challenged. There is a common sense and popular affect within the multiracial British working class of who they would side with in the story of David and Goliath; as Akram Salhab writes, 'it is impossible to envisage our own liberation outside a vision of international liberation'.

Imagining (and building) the politically impossible is certainly a form of denying the conservative vision of politics, but that denial does not preclude the possibility – I would argue necessity – of pragmatism. Aimé Césaire, the anti-colonial poet and politician, demonstrated throughout his life that liberatory politics are in fact well matched with pragmatism. Gary Wilder, discussing Césaire's dedication to pragmatism as a philosophical observance, explains that this was not about compromise or opportunism, as pragmatism is commonly understood, but a commitment to a non-dogmatic and experimental approach regarding the means to the ends: the recognition that making the politically impossible the politically inevitable is a dynamic process with few pre-existing formulas.[20] The Northern Police Monitoring Project, in Chapter 2 exploring the praxis of revolutionary abolitionist politics, suggests that this often looks like fighting for strategic reforms, as 'not all reforms are equal'. Thinking as a revolutionary and acting as one are two different sets of requirements.

How might this pragmatism guide us in thinking through the construction of an alliance of forces? Antiracism from above is evidenced in the proliferation of programmes in civic engagement – a strategy of assimilation – an equation in which civic power has become a stand-in for grassroots people power, the kind of power which seeks to fundamentally upturn the social order, root and branch. While building 'grassroots power' is spoken about across a number of chapters, whether it's No More Exclusions (by way of Stuart Hall) speaking about 'building where we are' or Sisters Uncut arguing that we 'wrestle liberation from the hands of the powerful by building grassroots power', it is also imperative that we reckon with both how much power we have and how – should we raise more power – it will be leveraged productively. Creating an alliance of forces in this moment of historic retreat for progressives will require the drawing together of a broad church. As Harnecker wrote, in the face of neoliberalism, we must 'unite all those who can be united'.[21]

* * *

It is almost impossible to say what will succeed in altering the balance of forces, but we can say what hasn't. It is true of this new millennium, as Vincent Bevins vividly illustrates in his recent book, *If We Burn*, that in the last two decades a surge of mass protest movements has electrified politics globally, toppling governments and invigorating embattled workers movements from Brazil to Egypt,[22] and most recently in Sudan and Sri-Lanka, often offering up a generation of clear-eyed political leaders from the grassroots. It is also true that the forms of left-wing party-political organisation preceding the new millennium has proven itself no longer up to the task. What feels increasingly self-evident to most of us who have participated in the eclectic mass protest movements of the early 2010s is that we need something between the vigorous, nimble, horizontal, mass protest movements and the disciplined, directed, programmatic, mass-member organisations of the past.

In the decades preceding this conjuncture, as Marta Harnecker notes, 'in each and every country, albeit in different ways, popular movements and not political parties were at the forefront of the struggle against neoliberalism'.[23] Looking specifically at experiences within Latin America, where neoliberal programmes were first launched into the world through blood and fire, Harnecker's reflections, best articulated in a series of essays entitled *Ideas for the Struggle* – while noting that there are not transhistorical, transnational solutions – have become a prognosis for most of the world, offering important and transferable lessons. Perhaps most notably, Harnecker wagers that for an alliance of grassroots and social forces to effectively come together they will need to wield a political 'instrument'; whether it is an existing apparatus such as a political party or something entirely new, it will need to be for us, by us and accountable to us. What kind of instrument can grassroots antiracist movements build to leverage their power for effective political gains?

Within the big picture of racial capitalism and super-exploitation, there is only a gradation of losers, be they Black, Brown or white, working class, or any other social class feeling the pinch. The fight against racism and racial capitalism is not supposed to be fought, or even led, solely by racialised people, it is for every movement, every progressive person, to recognise that they have a vital role. Unity, more than anything, is what frightens the political establishment. That said, if the history of resistance to racial capitalism teaches us anything, it is that from 1943 Warsaw to 1967 Detroit, liberation from within the capitalist ghettos, slums and hinterlands poses one of the most incendiary threats to business as usual. Self-organised struggles for emancipation from capitalism's edge-lands is the forerunner of resistance to its emergence and has been at the front line ever since. Before and alongside the ghettos there were the shipyards and maroon towns – eighteenth/nineteenth-century Mauritius, where my family hails from, a purpose-built colony and one of capitalism's early industrial world-engines, was regarded by sailors as a Maroon Republic,[24] the enclaves of Maroons on neighbouring Reunion island were known as the 'Kingdom of the Interior'. These were places where defiant anti-colonial communities raided plantation owners so frequently from their mountain enclaves that slave owners were at a loss as to how to contain the insurgencies. Later that century enslaved communities would band together under the leadership of Toussaint Louverture and defeat the Spanish, French and British in liberating Haiti. The earliest organised labour struggles emerged in the dockyards of the world, the merchant ship decks being themselves the earliest prototype of a factory. Indeed, the word *strike* as a form of industrial action literally meant to strike the sails so ships could no longer be launched, and these poor ship-workers, often paupers who were banded up and forced to work, took inspiration from the slave revolts.[25]

This emancipatory tradition, which appropriated the Enlightenment's clarion calls of universal freedom and gave it real life, is alive in the chapters present in this book. These contributors are the descendants of this tradition, shattering the illusions of business as usual by any means necessary. From them we have much to learn, much to refine and much to further.

1
Transforming Education

No More Exclusions

No More Exclusions (NME) is an intergenerational, Black-led, anti-racist coalition working to build a grassroots abolitionist movement in education. We seek to end the persistent race disparities in school exclusions and to effect change in policy, practice and culture within education and society as a whole. Our coalition includes ordinary people from all walks of life: young people, parents, advocates, educators, trade unionists, social workers, lawyers, youth workers, local councillors, journalists, radical scholars, special educational needs and disabilities (SEND) specialists, psychologists and mental health practitioners. We are united by our grave concern about school exclusions and the increasing lack of liberatory education within the UK and globally. Our ultimate goal is to end all forms of school exclusion and segregated education, and to develop free, inclusive and accessible education that liberates all learners.

We ask you to engage actively with this chapter, and to consider what changes you can make in your school, university, workplace or community. We don't claim to have all the answers, but we hope these ideas will encourage readers to join us in the struggle to dismantle the systems and everyday practices that push children and young people to the margins of society and to reimagine education as a lifelong, collective, emancipatory project.

Here we outline our theory of change, developed through a series of roundtables with affected young people, parents and carers, educators and researchers, held in summer 2022. We hope it captures some of the richness of these conversations, in which we reflected on our collective mission, vision and values.

Historical Movements that Inspire NME's Principles

We thank the elders, Bernard Coard, Professor Gus John and Eric and Jessica Huntley for their work. We accept the baton, and continue the fight for racial justice in education in the hope that we don't have to pass it onto the next generation.[1]

Our work builds on centuries of anti-colonial and Black radical resistance to systemic violence enacted against oppressed communities – from matrifocal networks of care in the Caribbean to youth-led literacy programmes in Cuba. More specifically, we are part of Britain's ongoing Black Parents and Black Education Movements, originated by Black radical parents, publishers, educators and activists such as John La Rose, Eric and Jessica Huntley, Bernard and Phyllis Coard, and Gus John. In the post-war period, Black parents, educators and community members came to understand that British education was not the route to social mobility they once hoped it would be. Bernard Coard's 1971 pamphlet, *How the West Indian Child Is Made Educationally Sub-normal in the British School System*, revealed the racist policies and practices that were designed to oppress Black pupils. This included the state's systematic labelling of Black Caribbean children as 'educationally subnormal', their abandonment in so-called dustbin schools and 'bussing' to schools outside their local communities.[2] It was in this context that racialised communities rose up to resist the school system's deliberate neglect and marginalisation of their children. Up and down the country, they led anti-banding and anti-bussing campaigns, such as the Haringey anti-banding campaign (1968–71), in which Black parents, educators and community members successfully challenged the council's racist attempts to push their children out of local schools and galvanised communities of colour to take action in localities across the country.[3] Children took part in student strikes, and educators established radical educational spaces in their homes in the form of Black supplementary schools whose curricula centred on Pan-African histories and cultures alongside global anti-colonial and anti-imperialist movements.[4] Similarly, under Altheia Jones-LeCointe's leadership, the British Black Panthers' community education programmes supported young Black people to understand (and resist) the links between educational exclusion and their experiences of policing and incarceration. These forms of everyday, collective organising armed many children with the political education they needed to survive what Hazel Carby terms 'schooling in Babylon'.[5] This focus on liberatory political education similarly underpins the seminal teachings of Brazilian educator Paulo Freire, whose concept of critical pedagogy runs throughout NME's work.

Like Freire, we oppose the traditional educational model which discourages critical thinking, reproduces social and economic inequalities, and situates students as passive vessels for teachers to fill with knowledge. Critical pedagogy is an emancipatory teaching tool that seeks to raise learners' 'critical consciousness' by encouraging them to reflect on the unjust, unequal and contradictory status quo, while supporting them to change these oppressive conditions through action.[6]

These historical movements (and many more) help us to see how the education system is not broken but is serving its deliberate purpose of maintaining, reproducing and exacerbating the unjust status quo. At the same time, they bolster our belief that we have the collective power to upend the violent systems and structures that seek to hold us down.

> When children attend schools that place a greater value on discipline and security than on knowledge and intellectual development, they are attending prep schools for prison.[7]

Our schools have become sites of punishment, where working-class racialised children are taught their (marginal) place in British society. Schools exert social control through suspensions and expulsions, excluding Black Caribbean children at a rate five times higher than their white counterparts.[8] Reflecting the demonisation and policing of Black children's conduct, Department for Education figures show that the most common reason for exclusion is 'persistent disruptive behaviour', with this included as a reason in over half (55 per cent) of all suspensions in the 2022–3 autumn term.[9] Teachers are more likely to label global majority, poor and disabled children as 'disruptive', thereby reinforcing racist, classist and ableist hierarchies.[10] These stereotypes compound marginalised children's risk of punishment, thus perpetuating false and harmful narratives that they are less capable and don't belong in the school community.[11] The NME members involved in our youth group roundtable cited teachers' perceptions in labelling them as 'challenging', 'difficult', 'rude' and 'bad' as fundamentally shaping their school and later life experiences. Indeed, the overwhelming feelings of powerlessness, isolation and abandonment caused by the deficit-laden labelling and exclusion of children can cause lifelong harm and trauma. At our roundtable, one young person shared: 'I'm 20 now. And I'm still remembering how I felt at school. I'm having those same feelings in other non-school specific situations. And I wouldn't feel those feelings if I wasn't excluded from school before.'

Racialised school exclusions are also enacted through discriminatory school policies, including those that enable the routine punishment and policing of Black children's hair, as experienced by Ruby Williams, who was excluded because her natural afro was 'too big'. Ruby's mum, Kate, shared with the parents' roundtable: 'people might think, "oh, it's only hair", but actually sometimes that's how it starts'. Indeed, the routine punishment of Black children's hair, which is rooted in white supremacist notions of what is 'normal' and 'acceptable', sends a loud, clear message about who does and doesn't belong in the school community. Nonetheless, the success of Ruby's case at the Equality and Human Rights Commission and the campaign against afro hair discrimination that has flourished as a result show that, with fire in their bellies, pupils and their parents are a force to be reckoned with.[12]

It's this type of patriarchal, white supremacist school culture that Pimlico Academy pupils rose up against in 2021, when their head teacher instituted uniform policies banning 'colourful' hijabs and hairstyles that 'block the views of others'. Pupils also challenged the flying of the union flag on school grounds, the erasure of British histories of race, migration and empire from the curriculum, and the school's silence on the Black Lives Matter movement. Though young NME members who participated in the uprising expressed disappointment that their school failed to deal with its issues from the root, the significance of their resistance can't be overstated. The school's head eventually resigned as a result of this powerful expression of collective pupil power.[13]

Through our organising, we seek to disrupt and dismantle the cycles of punishment, harm and exclusion on which the school-to-prison nexus is founded. Schools have increasingly become sites of oppression for working-class children of colour, who are surveilled by school-based police officers, CCTV, metal detectors, fingerprint biometrics and teachers who are under pressure to refer pupils who may be 'at risk of radicalisation' to Prevent, and to report those deemed 'at risk of involvement with gangs' directly to the police.[14] Cases such as the Metropolitan Police officers' strip search of 15-year-old Child Q at her Hackney school reflect the immense harm caused by bringing the legal system into schools. Meanwhile, excluded children are placed in highly securitised pupil referral units (PRUs) where they receive a rudimentary education and are vulnerable to exploitation.[15] Much like 'educationally subnormal' schools, PRU environments aren't equipped to support pupils to develop their talents or abilities, as is their right.

Reflecting the gendered and racialised implications of these exclusionary policies and practices, over half of the boys imprisoned in Young Offender Institutions are from a Black or global majority background;[16] meanwhile, over 60 per cent of England and Wales' adult prison population has experienced school exclusion.[17] This is the result of a system which excludes vulnerable individuals and scapegoats marginalised communities rather than dealing with the root causes of complex social issues.

After more than a decade of public spending cuts, and against the backdrop of intensifying health, climate and economic crises, the

Ministry of Justice (MoJ) is working to create 20,000 more prison places through the 'biggest prison building programme in more than 100 years'. This includes the introduction of 'secure schools' – children's prisons run by academy trusts and accountable to the MoJ.[18] Working-class global majority young people will likely meet the demand to fill these new places in the carceral state, having been systematically criminalised through racialised initiatives such as harsher sentencing rules, Manchester's new £2.5 million 'super-court-room' for large-scale 'gang' trials, and Knife Crime Prevention Orders. We don't need any further evidence to conclude that the state is waging an out-and-out war against our young people.[19]

Osime Brown and Jaden Moodie's mums joined our parents roundtable. Osime is a Black, autistic young man with high support needs. Osime's school excluded him when he was 16. He was forcibly taken into care, where social services moved him 28 times. In 2018, he was arrested and imprisoned under the 'joint enterprise' doctrine for the theft of a mobile phone – an offence he didn't commit. Because his sentence exceeded 12 months in prison, he lost his leave to remain in the UK (under the 2007 Borders Act); the Home Office prepared to deport him to Jamaica, a country he hadn't set foot in since he was four. Meanwhile, the serious case review into the murder of 14-year-old Jaden identified his exclusion from school as having contributed to his vulnerability to exploitation, which led to his premature and violent death. Jaden's bereaved mother, Jada, indicted the system as being 'designed to destroy our children'.

We continue to organise in solidarity with the Justice for Osime Brown campaign and support Jada's calls to introduce Jaden's Law, which would seek to stop schools excluding children without arranging appropriate alternative provision.[20] These harrowing cases reflect the central role of exclusions in the social, spiritual and even physical death of our children and young people. As Osime's mum Joan Martin stated: 'You can't harm children to that degree and then turn around and expect them to want to participate in society'. This is why we organise.

Through the choices we are making about our lives and the values which we are imparting to our children, we are making it clear that in whatever ways the society tries to constrain us, we will break free.[21]

Black Feminism

We organise as intersectional Black feminists who struggle against the ways that interlocking systems of oppression such as racism, sexism, poverty, ableism, homophobia and transphobia impact our lives.[22] We organise in the spirit of the Combahee River Collective, who understood that our collective liberation demands the dismantling of *all* oppressive systems, starting with capitalism, imperialism and patriarchy.[23] As Audre Lorde puts it: 'There is no such thing as a single-issue struggle because we do not live single-issue lives.'[24]

Centring the Most Marginalised

Our work seeks to centre the most marginalised at all times. Working-class Black Caribbean, mixed white and Black Caribbean, and Gypsy, Roma and Traveller pupils (particularly those with SEND) are hugely overrepresented in school exclusion numbers. They are the most marginalised, and they hold the greatest expertise on the issues impacting their lives. Therefore, our organising must prioritise and centre their experiences.

Grassroots Struggle

Our work is guided by cultural theorist Stuart Hall's assertion that 'we struggle where we are'. This means that we seek to enact change where and in whatever way we have the power to do so (be that in our schools, workplaces or communities). For educators, this could mean refusing to enact the school's discriminatory policies, while pupils and parents can harness their collective power to challenge harmful school policies and cultures.

We organise nationally through local, Black-led chapters. We believe that organising as members of the local community, and focusing on local issues, is key to impactful organising.

Flat Organisational Structure

We've adopted elements of the sociocracy governance model, meaning there's no formal hierarchy. Everyone can contribute existing skills or build new ones, and anyone can propose and implement an action. This helps to distribute power, knowledge and capacity, and makes NME a fluid organism with a constant flow of new ideas and fresh energy. We reach decisions by group majority consent, but young people and families with experience of exclusion always have the final say.

Abolition

NME is an abolitionist movement. As one member declared at the educators roundtable: 'When we say no more exclusions, we mean NO MORE EXCLUSIONS! We don't want reform, or to make exclusions less damaging or less disproportionate. We want to end all forms of exclusion.' Indeed, decades of reforms claimed to mitigate the harms caused by exclusion have actually exacerbated existing inequalities in the system and reinforced Britain's racialised class structure.[25]

In the context of education, abolition is twofold: doing away with systems and practices that push young people further into harm's way, and creating conditions in which all children can feel safe, supported and inquisitive. This means providing appropriate mental health and youth support services and real opportunities that inspire young people to pursue their passions and talents. This also means ensuring that the basic needs of young people and their communities are met through food security, decent housing and freedom from the border regime. We acknowledge that existing 'safeguarding' institutions have great capacity to reproduce racialised harms.

This is why NME's healing spaces, Kids of Colour's Manchester-based youth spaces, Black Learning Achievement and Mental Health UK's Zuri therapy sessions and 4Front's Jahiem's Justice Centre are so vital. They centre the healing of marginalised young people and exist beyond the reach of the carceral state.

Schools tend to default to exclusions to manage what they perceive as 'disruptive' and 'difficult' behaviour, without looking into its root causes. As one young member contended:

> It's important to have our emotional needs met, to make sure we're heard, to make sure we can talk about things. It's a shame that, when we raise concerns in the education system or when we act in a certain way, teachers or adults or whoever is around us in the school environment, consider us to be acting inappropriately rather than looking at the causes and trying to understand 'okay, why are you acting this way?'

Children and young people need support to deal with the complex issues that impact their lives, not punishment. Consequences don't have to mean exclusion, and exclusions don't facilitate accountability.[26] They don't offer justice, care or safety for anyone involved. We need whole-school and whole-society approaches that deal with the root causes of harm.[27]

Accountability

We aim to support members to be accountable, to identify ways the collective can support them to remain involved and to address patterns of behaviour that don't align with our values. We don't believe in a one-size-fits-all approach to fostering transformative justice and accountability, but approaches can include: facilitating reflection, accountability or healing circles; resourcing appropriate counselling; taking a break from organising to work on self-reflection; engaging in dialogue and attempting to come up with solutions together and how the member intends to take action in addressing the behaviours in question; and creating a plan to support the member to remain in the movement.

This accountability process demands mutual trust, which is a core organising principle. Our communities have historically been let down by those in power, and our movements have been systematically disrupted by infiltrators (from the United States' infamous fifteen-year Counter Intelligence Program aimed at subverting radical political organisations in the 1960s to the more recent SpyCops).[28] We can't build a sustainable movement if we can't trust each other.

Our Strategic Approach

We developed our strategy by examining and drawing lessons from past struggles for Black liberation. We stay responsive to the ever-evolving landscape by monitoring current and future developments in education policy, research and practice. While the strategy group meets on a monthly basis, NME meets annually as a collective to set the year's strategic agenda and come together as a community to refocus, learn, grow, break bread and share joy. In January 2023, NME members came together for a weekend in Bristol, where the full membership contributed to strategic thinking, planning and execution.

NME has five main organising strands: Youth Voice and Development; Parent and Carer Partnerships; Curriculum Change; Educator Care; Research, Law and Policy. Each strand has a degree of autonomy, and develops strategies around membership, solidarity and political education in relation to the unique challenges they confront.

Research

We engage in the Black feminist praxis of 'speaking back' to those in power by producing and sharing what one member described as 'agitational research'. Our evidence-based arguments seek to counter the prevailing exclusions narrative which blames marginalised children for the schooling experiences that traumatise them and purposefully obscures the ways in which the British state and its institutions have actively curtailed global majority children's educational opportunities.

At the height of the Covid-19 pandemic, we produced research challenging the assumption that, because most pupils weren't in class, exclusions weren't happening. We found similar patterns of disproportionalities in exclusions happening throughout the pandemic, as well as concerning new categories of exclusions, such as 'failure to comply with COVID regulations'.[29]

Through our research, we disseminate knowledge beyond the reach of those in power and put it to work against them. We democratise knowledge the state seeks to obscure by producing research collaboratively and making it accessible to a broad audience – from creating clear guidance to help parents challenge school exclusions, to contributing to 'Holding Our Own', a collaboratively produced guide to non-policing solutions to serious youth violence[30] and Maslaha's radical safeguarding guidebook.[31] Our strategic approach to research also means foregrounding some of the many alternatives to exclusion. Our radical guidebook, 'What About the Other 29', is a seminal piece of research to this end, in which we set out a constellation of alternatives in policy and practice.[32] This has already made a tangible difference, with educators approaching us to say that they have implemented some of these lessons in their classrooms. Building on this, we're working with Abolitionist Futures to develop a more thorough set of practical alternatives to exclusion, demystifying potential courses of action in an imagined world where exclusion is not an option.

Law and Policy

Our research underpins our campaigns, policy recommendations and work lobbying government ministers, MPs and local councillors. Our key policy demands include: a moratorium on school exclusions; the removal of police from schools; and an end to internal exclusions.

Part of our core strategy has been to build power and force systemic change through education union organising. With our co-conspirators, we managed to achieve a 94 per cent vote in favour of a moratorium on school exclusions at the National Education Union's 2021 conference. The following year saw a vote in favour of removing police from schools.[33] Since these significant wins, however, right-wing forces within the union have used their power to marginalise NME and our demands, banning us from hosting a stall at the 2023 conference. This exclusionary approach is perhaps not surprising from a union labelled as institutionally racist by its own staff and members.[34] However, recognising the political power unions still hold, we must continue to strategically engage with them, while insisting on stronger antiracist policies and practices when it comes to school exclusions.

One of our key successes has been the mainstreaming of our ideas. Five years ago, very few people were talking about school exclusions and racialised disparities in exclusion rates, let alone the idea of ending this form of punishment altogether. With our allies, we've managed to push these ideas into mainstream consciousness, creating changes in education policy, practice and intellectual production. Initiatives such as Southwark Council's commitment to stopping exclusions in the borough, the Runnymede Trust's call for the removal of police from schools and a moratorium on exclusions, and former Children's Commissioner Anne Longfield's call to end primary school exclusions all show an increasing appetite for change. Meanwhile, in Hackney, Councillor Anntoinette Bramble announced a pilot of no Year 7 exclusions following the devastating, violent death of 15-year-old Tashaûn Aird, whose exclusion acted as a 'catalyst' for the exploitation which led to his premature death.[35] These commitments fall very short of our abolitionist demands but demonstrate the penetration of our arguments into the mainstream. In order to achieve our vision, we need *most* members of society to recognise that the violence of exclusion is unconscionable. This demands cultural transformation – change which cannot be achieved through policy and legislation alone.

Fostering Solidarity

Our coalition-building work is central to our organising strategy. This is based on our understanding that struggles around police and prisons, the climate, migration, physical and mental health care, housing, food and land are all interconnected. We organise in coalition with other grassroots groups and campaigns such as 4Front's work ending the strip search of children and Alliance for Inclusive Education and Disabled Black Lives Matter's work towards disability justice, as well as those demanding climate justice as part of the climate reparations bloc at COP26. It is essential that we work collectively to nurture a politics of care in each aspect of our everyday lives and create a world in which no one is disposable. It is imperative that we form intersectional alliances to build a broad base of power.

Vision

A world without exclusions would be a world where people aren't living in poverty, where people have access to housing, where people have all the basic necessities, where you don't have a culture of violence, where you're eradicating and uprooting all of these structural oppressions. Everything has to shift.[36]

As one member explained, we envision a world 'in which all children and young people feel safe, free, celebrated, loved, included and supported to thrive'. This demands an education system with no form of exclusion or segregation – one that doesn't depend on punishment, discipline or policing. This means no isolation booths; no suspensions or expulsions; no PRUs; no police in schools, and no 'secure schools' (or children's prisons); and no more exclusionary school policies and curricula. These are all tools of social control, and they ultimately make schools sites for punishment and criminalisation instead of safety, learning and creativity.

Instead, we envision an education system that empowers and liberates learners by giving them the tools they need to change the world for the better. This means collaborative, lifelong education that supports agency and encourages young people to build community; schools that centre healing and transformative approaches and encourage growth through accountability; an education that is unconditional and values each and every pupil and educator; a curriculum that reflects the complex world we live in and respects multiple ways of knowing, learning and being; liberatory pedagogies that help students to understand and address the root causes of harm in our schools and society. This is an education system in which exclusion is unthinkable.

Our vision for the world is simple: a world in which everyone's basic needs are met. In this transformed world, we prioritise connection, healing and care, ensuring the most vulnerable and marginalised people in society are put first. How we get there is a little more complicated and demands our collective efforts. Change is rarely linear or immediately visible, but nonetheless change is coming. We are excited about the future of antiracist organising and hope that this book encourages more young people, parents, educators and community members to make change where they are. Our hope for a future in which we can all thrive does not lie with the state and its carceral institutions but in the collective, everyday activism of ordinary people. Though it may feel incredibly distant, this future is possible, necessary and urgent.

2

Monitoring, Non-reformist Reforms, Solidarity, Internationalism and Abolitionist Dreams

The Northern Police Monitoring Project

Part of a long history of resistance to racist policing,[1] the Northern Police Monitoring Project (NPMP) was formed in 2012 in South Manchester.[2] The project emerged following several flashpoints, including the police harassment of Somali-run cafes and individuals. While the particular sparks that ignited NPMP came in 2012, as founding member Tanzil Chowdhury has argued, 'tensions between Greater Manchester Police (GMP) and local communities began well before',[3] with a long and unrelenting history of police harassment, violence and stigmatisation, particularly targeting working-class, migrant and racially minoritised communities. This history of police violence has been matched by an equally long tradition of grassroots resistance dating back to the nineteenth century and the spontaneous street-level protests of Manchester's overpoliced and underprotected Irish and early African migrant communities, which mobilised at different historical junctures to defend themselves from racist attacks and unjust policing practices.[4] By the mid-twentieth century, community resistance became increasingly organised, with radicals such as pan-Africanist Ras Makonnen and communist Len Johnson taking inspiration from the US-based International Labor Defense in fundraising and supporting the legal campaigns of those who faced injustice at the hands of the police and court system in Manchester and beyond. In his memoir, Makonnen – who in 1946 famously secured the services of Jamaica's leading lawyer, Norman Manley, to represent Donald Beard, a Jamaican RAF serviceman accused of murdering a white man in Fallowfield, Manchester – would describe 'this defense business [as] almost a daily concern' during the post-war period.[5] These foundational campaigns established a pedagogy of resistance in the form of the 'defence committee',[6] which would be continued by subsequent generations of local activists, including those working through Manchester-based branches of Black Power formations such as the Universal Coloured People's Association, the Black Unity and Freedom Party, the Asian Youth Movement and the Black Parents Movement. The last of these formed a series of high-profile defence committees throughout the late 1970s and 1980s, including for Jackie Berkeley who accused GMP officers of sexual assault following her arrest and detention at Moss Side Police Station in April 1984.[7]

As founding members Joanna Gilmore and Waqas Tufail have written, NPMP emerged to act 'as a forum from which individuals, groups and communities can collectively challenge corrupt policing practices and monitor instances of police violence and harassment', to provide 'a genuine challenge to the official narrative on crime and policing'.[8] NPMP was therefore founded upon a three-pronged approach that included signposting individuals to legal support and representation, supporting local and regional campaigns, and developing a programme for training community members in street-level monitoring.[9] From its inception to the present day, NPMP operates entirely independently from the police and other state agencies. This principle of independence is born in part from a recognition of 'the dangers of relying on institutions of the state to self-regulate',[10] demonstrated by the systemic failure of public bodies – from the Independent Office of Police Conduct (formerly the Independent Police Complaints Commission) to official misconduct hearings, review panels, inquests and the courts – to secure truth, justice and accountability for those affected by racist policing. Through maintaining our independence from the police, we also seek to demonstrate our commitment to building and maintaining community trust and organisational security.

In recent years, as the group has changed shape and grown, NPMP's work has changed too – most notably expanding to focus on Greater Manchester more broadly, rather than its initial hyperlocal work. Street-level monitoring has given way to a greater focus on casework and other forms of monitoring and information gathering. Although the threads were perhaps always there, abolitionist politics has also become increasingly explicit in its centrality to our thinking, strategy and actions. In recent years, we have been involved in work on several specific issues and campaigns, each at varying stages and with varying levels of intensity. Formed in 2020, following increasing concern from community members and a Freedom of Information request finding that GMP planned to introduce more officers to Greater Manchester's schools, the No Police in Schools[11] campaign has been the most high profile and time intensive of these. We also, as part of Resistance Lab,[12] worked to develop a report and resources calling for the abolition of Tasers,[13] and most recently we have worked with bereaved families to draw attention to the growing issue of police killings through police pursuits.[14]

In this chapter, we focus primarily on our work on these three issues/campaigns, as we consider (1) the importance of monitoring, casework and independence; (2) the abolitionist concept of non-reformist reforms; (3) the importance of multiracial and multigenerational coalitions; (4) internationalism; and (5) abolitionist dreams.

Monitoring, Casework and Independence

Police monitoring and casework are core components of NPMP's work. Monitoring involves collecting information about the police and then processing that information in some way, often to reveal patterns in policing that can inform our work and/or that of other organisations within the local, national or international ecosystem of resistance. Initially, NPMP arranged for volunteers to be trained as legal observers who could then engage in street monitoring in two areas of Manchester: Hulme and Moss Side. In recent years, however, we have adopted a more expansive conceptualisation of police monitoring. In part this decision was made for practical reasons: the extension of NPMP's remit from South Manchester to the whole of Greater Manchester made it difficult to sustain targeted street monitoring across the county. But it was also based on a recognition that the harms of policing are (increasingly) not only confined to the street, with policing reaching into our schools and workplaces,[15] operating in partnership with a growing number of state and non-state agencies and becoming ever more data driven.[16] Our current monitoring work is therefore multifaceted, with the street-level monitoring being maintained at key overpoliced events such as Caribbean Carnival, and other elements growing through, for example, our monitoring of state proceedings.

Being driven by the views and experiences of affected communities is a key principle that informs our monitoring work. We engage with affected communities to seek testimonies about police encounters. We listen to the accounts of community members at our public events, in private meetings with individuals and families, and via email, social media and our online reporting form. These testimonies alert us to key issues affecting local communities and, over time, allow us to observe patterns or changes in policing. For example, it was listening to young people, teachers, youth workers and other community members at an event on the school-to-prison pipeline – co-hosted with Kids of Colour in 2020 – that alerted us to issues concerning the presence of police in Greater Manchester schools, which in turn functioned as a catalyst for the No Police in School Campaign. Furthermore, with permission, we also keep a log of community members' encounters with the police, which will allow us – as the log grows – to challenge GMP's data and the narrative that they tell. Listening to affected communities is vital for resistance movements.

We also use other forms of monitoring to track patterns in policing. Freedom of Information requests, the monitoring of news stories, conducting our own public surveys and consultations, and analysing the state's own data, including use-of-force data, all play an important role in directing our strategy and determining campaigning priorities. It was through the monitoring of GMP via local news stories that we were alerted to a possible increase in fatalities following police pursuits in 2021–2, which we have since been able to confirm using data published by the Independent Office for Police Conduct (IOPC). Our work makes it clear that across all police forces, 'GMP were the worst offenders in a year when the number of road traffic fatalities involving police in England and Wales reached a four-year high'.[17] We are now working closely with affected families and loved ones to build a family-led campaign to End Police Pursuit. As well as using the knowledge gained through monitoring to inform campaigning, we also compile and publish our monitoring work as reports and statements with the aim of raising public awareness around police injustices and building our network of supporters and allies. The *Decriminalise the Classroom*[18] report on police in schools and our (bi)annual NPMP magazine[19] are key examples.

Our monitoring work operates in a symbiotic relationship with advocacy and casework. Through the various mechanisms outlined above, we identify or are approached by individuals and families that are affected by police violence, harassment and racism. We work with those individuals and families to: document police wrongdoing; support them to understand their legal rights; explore options for seeking redress, including by referring onto trusted solicitors; and offer emotional support as they navigate the challenging and often disappointing state processes. The last of these might involve attending key events, such as coroners' inquests or civil or criminal court cases, and taking notes, but as Clarke, Chadwick and Williams note, it also involves simply bearing witness: 'being present, being consistent, being approachable, being engaged and being a support'.[20] This is an essential, though less recognised, component of resistance work. While our approach to casework is primarily about supporting those directly affected by police injustice to have the confidence, skills and resources to advocate for themselves, through the act of bearing witness we are ourselves politically educated in the process around the experience and challenges encountered by those at the sharp end of state violence. In turn, this shapes our future organising strategies and campaigning: as A. Sivanandan,[21] the former director of the Institute of Race Relations, put it, transformative work turns 'cases into issues, issues into causes, and causes into a movement'.[22]

The principle of independence from the police, and the state more broadly, is fundamental to our casework but has also been foundational to NPMP's broader work since our formation. This means that we do not share a platform with the police: we will not, for example, act as a mediator between the police and the people that we support, nor will we participate in events to debate with police officers or sit on police advisory panels. This position is not unique but rather one commonly adopted by police monitoring groups and, as Netpol's Kevin Blowe notes, represents 'a conscious choice to take sides with local people experiencing injustices in their treatment by the police'.[23] It deliberately privileges the accounts of 'the policed' over the state narrative in an attempt to subvert dominant hierarchies of power and enable truth telling in a context in which victims of police harassment and violence are routinely disbelieved or silenced.[24] In so doing, we build trust with the bereaved families and overpoliced communities that we work with, fostering confidence that our advocacy and campaigning work will not be tempered by the state. It also ensures that we do not become complicit in the extension of police–community panels which function to create the illusion of accountability and diffuse people's anger',[25] while enabling the state to claim that it has the community's consent to extend policing.

Non-reformist Reforms

As we have increasingly come to identify ourselves explicitly as an abolitionist organisation, the concept of *non-reformist reforms*[26] (also known as *abolitionist reforms* or *abolitionist steps*) has been important in enabling us to navigate the apparent tensions between abolition as our long-term goal and the more incremental reforms that can be made in the shorter term as part of a politics of survival, pending abolition.[27] In the context of policing – where reformist reforms are those that add legitimacy, power or resources to the police (such as budget increases that seek to enable the police to better do their job) – non-reformist reforms are those that avoid strengthening the police, instead chipping away at and rolling back their power. Crucially, the concept reminds us that abolition and reform need not *necessarily* be seen as dichotomous or at odds. Instead, it offers us 'a way out of the binary opposition between reform and revolution'.[28] Moreover, cast against its antithesis concept of reformist reforms, non-reformist reforms show us that not all reforms are equal (not all constitute a surrender to the system). The pursuit of non-reformist reforms, and resistance to reformist reforms, is therefore a key principle in our work.

In practice, we have found that the distinction between reformist and non-reformist reforms often proves to be a fine line. Does our calling for the end of Taser use against children risk inadvertently legitimising and solidifying its use against adults, for example? Or does our calling for an end to police pursuits in circumstances involving suspicion of a nonviolent crime or minor traffic violation risk endorsing potentially deadly pursuits in other circumstances? Such questions are not easily answered. This is particularly true because it is not always possible to foresee the range of ways in which seemingly non-reformist reforms can be distorted and morph into reformist reforms, and because – when their hand is forced by campaigners – those in power are far more likely to create the illusion of change rather than actually make change.

The No Police in Schools campaign has been an interesting space that has given us occasion to think about non-reformist reforms, and from where we have drawn useful lessons as we put principles into practice. Fundamentally, we have come to think of the campaign's central demand for No Police in Schools as a non-reformist reform in the abolitionist movement against policing. The removal of police from schools rolls back the power and reach of the police and thus would take us closer towards the long-term goal of police abolition. Such an understanding allows us to see our campaign as part of a broader movement and fosters a sense of solidarity with a range of related campaigns. Part of our framing of No Police in Schools as a non-reformist reform is also based on our belief that if we can develop convincing arguments that police have no place in schools, then those arguments can be meaningfully and persuasively applied to other contexts, situations and campaigns, creating a ripple effect as our campaigning and organising becomes more refined through an ongoing feedback loop of theory and action. Relatedly, as we come to demonstrate that there are far more useful (or less harmful) ways to invest resources to support young people, then that logic can also be applied to other related contexts, which also feeds the longer-term goal of police abolition.

On a smaller scale, the non-reformist reform concept is something we have also frequently thought about *within* the campaign as we present our demands and arguments. We ask: what are the non-reformist reforms that guide us towards the goal of having no police in schools? It has enabled us to be clear that more training or more women or more people of colour in the roles of school-based police officers stand in the way of, rather than move us towards, our campaign goal of removing police from schools.[29] Such tweaks create the illusion of change, providing a veneer of legitimacy that attempts to insulate those in power from criticism while the power and presence of the police remains intact.

A more complex example came through what appeared to be a significant victory for the campaign. In 2021, following years of campaigning by the No Police in Schools group and a recent wave of action – including billboards, flyering and the release of a campaign video – Manchester City Council's lead for Children and Services sent an email to all city councillors notifying them that the council would be removing all current school-based police officers and additional planned school-based police officers would not be introduced. He cited community 'concerns about disproportionate policing and the impacts on racial inequality'.[30] At first glance, this certainly looked and felt like a victory. However, the councillor did provide a little more detail that prompted caution. This was not the simple removal of police from schools, he explained, but the introduction of a 'different model for the city' which had been developed through conversation with GMP. This model would see 'dedicated school engagement officers, one for each locality of north, central, south [Manchester] and a further officer who will concentrate on the city-wide PRU and alternative provision'.[31]

We were unsure of the extent to which this marked progress or a victory for us as a campaign, though we agreed that much more work still needed to be done. While none of us felt that it was *the* victory, some thought it was a step forwards – that it made a material difference that police would no longer be placed directly in schools. Some of us felt that the publicity and high-level criticism of police was a good thing too and that, even if the positives were only very partial, it was important to celebrate this as a victory. A more critical reading, though (which many of us have come to over time), saw this as little more than a rearrangement of the furniture, or a *reformist reform* that did not peel back the power of the police but rather thwarted resistance and opposition through the illusion of change, while perhaps bringing the police into the lives of more young people across more schools. In fact, as the councillor said in his email, while Manchester had previously had three school-based officers working at four Manchester high schools, this arrangement would see five officers working across many schools: that is, two additional officers, and many more affected schools and young people.

We have found a guide for evaluating reforms from Mariame Kaba, a US abolitionist organiser and educator, helpful at various junctures and particularly in instances described above. The guide, though brief, offers a useful basis for organisations developing their own ways of ensuring their work is non-reformist. The opening two questions from Kaba are instructive here:

1. Are the proposed reforms allocating more money to the police? If yes, then you should oppose them.
2. Are the proposed reforms advocating for MORE police and policing (under euphemistic terms like 'community policing' run

out of regular police districts)? If yes, then you should oppose them.[32]

On both counts, our apparent victory is cast in doubt. We know that increases in the number of school-based police officers under the previous model were due, and that – amid national increases – these increases have come to pass.[33] However, we do not know exactly how many officers were to be introduced to Manchester Central and therefore do not know whether the increase in funding or officers under the new model was greater or less than that which we would have seen under the old model. Regardless of the answer here, it would be difficult to claim this as an *unambiguous* step towards abolition or a (*clear*) non-reformist reform. At best, it offers a marginal improvement (making the police a less central and permanent fixture of the lives of some students), and at worst it further solidifies the presence of police in schools through a veneer of legitimacy and the performance of responding to community concerns. It perhaps slowed us down as a campaign group too: we have grappled with how we now adapt our work to respond to the fact that – nominally at least – there are no longer school-based police officers in Manchester. How could we mobilise against a threat that the council had performed away? This example offers an important lesson with regard to how non-reformist demands can be distorted into more reformist interventions by the state. Resistance movements must be vigilant in this regard.

Solidarity and the Building of Multiracial and Cross-generational Coalitions

As a police-monitoring organisation, much of our day-to-day activity is focused on supporting people directly affected by state violence, connecting them with others that have shared experiences and building issue-based campaigns capable of challenging dominant state narratives. Our Steering Committee members come to this work from different backgrounds and identities, but they are increasingly bound together by shared commitments to an abolitionist future, the realisation of which hinges on 'working with and through difference' to sustain mass movements for change.[34]

This politics of solidarity grows out of shared ideology but also our everyday encounters with the complex ways in which interlocking systems of imperialist, white supremacist, capitalist patriarchy inform the violence enacted by policing on the ground against differently situated people and communities.[35] For example, our experiences in the No Police in Schools campaign have shown us that, mirroring wider patterns in policing (and who gets policed), police are more likely to be assigned to schools in working-class communities, and that due to institutionalised racism in both policing and educational settings, Black and other racialised populations are disproportionately vulnerable to their presence. As we outlined in our *Decriminalise the Classroom* report, 'Safer Schools' initiatives are driven in large part by the racialised moral panic surrounding 'gangs' and serve to exacerbate the impact of counter-terror initiatives such as the Prevent duty which disproportionately impact Muslim and South Asian students.[36] Our report and public meetings also revealed the concerns of young people and youth workers regarding the presence of police in schools that renders other groups vulnerable, including women and girls, and LGBTQ+ and disabled people. We concluded that while 'police in schools are a problem for us all, it is vital that we recognise that some will be more affected than others'.[37] Understanding issues in this way is central to our values because it enables us to recognise complexity and (potentially) shared experiences (all may be affected) that can breed resistance, while also not erasing the way that power dynamics operate (some are affected more than others). This is a fine balance, but on both of these counts (failure to recognise the shared, failure to recognise the specific), many movements have failed in the past.

In each of our campaigns, we seek to adopt an evidence-based approach when reaching conclusions about the impact of various forms of police violence on differently situated groups. In our work on Tasers with Resistance Lab, we identified that Black people in

Greater Manchester were subject to the weapon's use at four times the rate of white people and that people with disabilities or suffering from mental health conditions were acutely vulnerable.[38] Our police pursuit campaign has shown that young working-class men and boys, disproportionately from Black, Brown and Gypsy, Roma and Traveller communities are most likely to lose their lives in the escalating crisis of pursuit-related deaths involving GMP.[39] Adopting this evidence-based approach to issue-led campaigning allows us to test our assumptions and be sensitive to the differential impact of police violence across particular groups in order to build inclusive campaigns. The use of evidence to inform where we're going should be a key value for justice movements.

In building our campaigns, we place a priority on centring (while not overexposing) those directly affected by police violence, racism and harassment at the same time as forging broad-based multiracial and cross-generational coalitions. The End Police Pursuits campaign is led by the loved ones of the young men and boys killed in police pursuits. As a result, it is a multiracial alliance akin to other family-led campaigns such as those against deaths in state custody by the United Families & Friends Campaign (UFFC) and joint enterprise convictions led by Joint Enterprise Not Guilty by Association. Our No Police in Schools campaign was created in partnership with the organisation Kids of Colour to ensure that the young people most affected by the presence of police in schools were actively involved from the outset. However, the campaign also involved representation from other groups that brought their own knowledge and power to the campaign, including parents, teachers, youth workers, academics, activists and other community members. Teachers associated with the National Education Union's (NEU) North-West Black Members Organising Forum played a critical role in passing 'no police in schools' motions in NEU branches across Greater Manchester; activists associated with Manchester Momentum, GM Tenants Unions and Acorn raised awareness among their networks and voted to affiliate with the campaign; and parents exerted pressure on head teachers and boards of governors for change. This, we hope, is an example of the principle of coalitional organising which we aspire to.

This form of multiracial and cross-generational coalition building has deep roots in earlier Manchester-based organising traditions, including many of the anti-deportation campaigns of the 1980s as well as the work of the Moss Side Defence Committee following the 1981 uprisings.[40] While the latter was Black-led, the committee worked to build solidarity between directly affected young people, their families and a wider network of political activists, trade unionists and radical lawyers. In a 2011 interview, Gus John, who served as chair of the committee, reflected on his hopes that this loose 'alliance' might become a 'mass movement' that worked collectively 'in pursuit of justice and against police brutality and harassment'.[41] We share these hopes in our own moment and continue to employ methods of multiracial and cross-generational coalition building to this end.

At the same time, we also recognise the importance of a broader form of cross- or intergenerational dialogue with the activists who came before us. The silencing, omission and erasure of the history of antiracist resistance to policing is a key weapon in the arsenal of those in power, disconnecting us from longer organising traditions that offer important lessons and inspiration in the present. For this reason, we have dedicated organisational time and resources to surfacing and critically engaging with these histories of resistance through our collective writing activities, public events and day-to-day strategy discussions, as well as through our own ongoing efforts to document and preserve NPMP's contributions for the generations that follow.[42]

The Global Dimensions of Policing and Abolitionist Solidarity

Our critical engagement with this longer history as well as contemporary abolitionist frameworks has underscored the importance of thinking across both time *and* space when building solidarity and movements against racist policing. Abolitionist thinkers have taught us that the birth of modern policing in the nineteenth century coincided with the rise of racial slavery, colonialism and waged labour and was designed 'to manage the consequences of [these global] regimes of exploitation'.[43] Britain's first police force was forged and tested in the colonial laboratory of Ireland before the fruits of this extraordinary expansion of state power ricocheted back to the metropole with the formation of the Metropolitan Police in 1829.[44] NPMP's co-founder, Tanzil Chowdhury, describes this process as a 'colonial boomerang' (following Michel Foucault, Aimé Césaire, Hannah Arendt and others) and cautions us to be attentive to the ways in which the violence of the imperial project 'continues to shape the technologies of British state violence today'.[45]

Resistance to policing in Manchester has always necessitated attention to this 'colonial boomerang'. During the 1981 Moss Side Uprisings, community members were confronted with police tactics drawn straight from the Royal Ulster Constabulary's playbook in Northern Ireland, including the controversial use of police vehicles by 'snatch squads' who sought to pull people directly off the streets as well as to disperse protestors by driving into crowds at high speeds.[46] More broadly, the legacies of empire are apparent in processes of racialisation, including what Jasbinder Nijjar describes as Britain's *enduring* racial project of 'constructing, controlling and punishing colonial subjects as criminal *collectives*'.[47] Nijjar shows us that the racial construction of 'the gang' has its roots in the colonial policing of Northern Ireland, Kenya and British-ruled India but continues to underpin strategies directed towards the policing of so-called 'gang crime as a Black phenomenon'.[48] These strategies, which also take cues from the globalisation of US-based 'gangs' policing, include the labelling of young Black men as 'gang members' with weak or non-existent evidence, the conflation of 'gangs' with serious youth violence and the building of racist 'gangs' databases culminating in overpolicing and unjust prosecutions often under racist joint enterprise or conspiracy laws.[49] Today, these racialised policing practices are intensified (and afforded an air of legitimacy) by the lucrative international market in new forms of high-tech surveillance, including facial recognition technologies, data-driven profiling and predictive policing tools in which 'discriminatory computer algorithms are employed to predict where crime will be committed and by whom'.[50]

NPMP's work in Greater Manchester takes place against the backdrop of the systematic use of these racist strategies against Black, migrant and working-class young people. In spring 2022, we were present as ten boys were found guilty by association for the crimes of conspiracy to commit murder and conspiracy to commit GBH with intent. No one was killed in this case and nearly 40 days in court revealed that the majority of those prosecuted were never involved in or accused of direct involvement in any violence. Rather, the prosecution deployed a racist 'gang' narrative, drawing upon their online relational networks, text messages, drill lyrics and Instagram videos to bind and implicate all ten in a criminal conspiracy. All are now serving lengthy prison sentences of between 8 and 20 years.[51] Later in the summer, we initiated a campaign against GMP's engagement in 'data-driven' profiling after learning that GMP's XCalibre 'gangs' task force (XTF) had issued letters to dozens of young people warning them not to attend the annual Manchester Caribbean carnival. Recipients had been identified, likely using the XTF's racist 'gangs' database, as either being 'a member of a street gang', 'affiliated to a street gang' or 'perceived by others to be associated to a street gang'.[52] A subsequent investigation by Novara Media revealed that hundreds of such letters had been issued since 2006 and that an overwhelming majority were given to Black people.[53] In 2023, after Kids of Colour and Liberty threatened legal action owing to the discriminatory nature of the carnival bans, GMP were forced to stop sending the letters for the 2023 carnival.[54]

In this context, effective organising necessitates transnational knowledge sharing and networks capable of equipping grassroots activists with the tools to comprehend the increasingly high-tech global landscape of contemporary policing strategies as well as the forms of resistance that have worked in the most affected areas around the world. In terms of knowledge sharing, we have learned a tremendous amount from US-based campaigners about Taser technology and the inherent risks of the weapon being rolled out to all front-line officers in England and Wales. Similarly, in our campaign to End Police Pursuit we have gained important strategic insights from more advanced campaigns in the USA and Australia which have fought to ban pursuits in circumstances where the driver is suspected of a nonviolent or minor traffic offence. We have also sought to build transnational partnerships with other abolitionist groups working actively around shared concerns and goals. In 2020, we began working with similar No Police in Schools campaigns in the United States, Scotland and Canada. In 2022, we also joined the Justice, Equity and Technology Table, which is dedicated to bringing together activists working to address the impacts of data-driven policing on racialised communities throughout Europe.[55] We've drawn lessons about the importance of internationalism in movements that have gone before us, and hope those that follow will take these lessons seriously too.

Abolitionist Dreams

As part of this wider local, national and international ecosystem of resistance, NPMP is also committed to collective abolitionist *freedom dreaming*[56] – that is, to proactively envisioning and creating new ways of responding to harm and inequality within our communities that are not based on carceral logics. This involves supporting existing and building new alternatives to the police. This strand of our work is built on the principle that abolition is not simply a 'negative process of tearing down' harmful institutions such as the police; rather it is one of 'reimagining institutions, ideas, and strategies, and creating new institutions'.[57] For example, a core strand of the No Police in Schools campaign works to build a more emancipatory education system that does not simply replace the police with seemingly more benign institutions that allow punishment and inequality to continue to operate, only in a more hidden fashion. With this in mind, we call for (school) budgets to be increased and allocated to more counsellors, youth workers and teachers, but at the same time we must work alongside other activist partners to ensure that those professions also undergo radical change. In that regard, we are led by and have learned much from groups such as Maslaha, who have developed a radical safeguarding resource for practitioners working in school contexts.[58] We also recognise that removing police from schools cannot happen in a vacuum and therefore we must do what we can to bolster the important work of groups such as No More Exclusions, and those such as Kids of Colour and 4Front, who are championing healing-centred approaches to the harms facing young people.

Part of our current work to build non-carceral alternatives involves reimagining mechanisms for holding the police to account. Much of our learning around this has come through working closely with families in Greater Manchester who have had loved ones killed in a police pursuit. Although the IOPC's lack of independence from the police has been a concern within activist circles for some time,[59] the experiences of the bereaved families that we are working with have reaffirmed that state processes offer little hope of justice. Moreover, they create the harmful illusion of accountability, and in so doing they placate and silence families seeking justice and exhaust families through lengthy delays, leaving them less able to pursue other forms of accountability. Coroners' inquests, for example, offer a hope that too often does not come to fruition, and instead families are left to navigate a process that is both alien and alienating, without any form of state-funded emotional support. In this context, we must, as a resistance movement, create our own structures to hold the state to account. One possible avenue for this is the People's Tribunal on Police Killings[60] announced at the UFFC march in 2021, which will highlight evidence from affected people to make a series of decisions that 'can then be implemented with the support of international bodies'. Simultaneously, we must grow our collective capacity to offer structures of support and care that, in turn, grow our collective capacity to resist.

The struggle continues.

Land as a Site of Antiracist Struggle

Land In Our Names

The injustices experienced by Black people and people of colour (BPOC) today are historically linked to the theft of land in Britain and Ireland, colonial expansion and the exploitation of former colonies through the creation of systems of capitalism and racism. These systems continue to shape who has access to material resources and whose belonging matters on this land today.

In turn, the beliefs guiding our work and ethos, as organisers engaged in the land justice movement today, emerge from resistance to the history of harms inherent in racist capitalist systems. Fundamentally, we believe that land cannot be owned, merely stewarded for both our ancestors and descendants.

Land in Our Names' members honour our diasporic experience as formerly colonised peoples, including by venerating the agricultural activities of our predecessors and ancestors in land struggles. These struggles are not always made visible in British antiracist movements, and antiracism has not historically been placed at the forefront of land justice movements in Britain.

The preceding centuries contain a wealth of international inspiration for present-day land struggles, including the revolt and burning of plantations by enslaved Africans, fugitivity and marronage (the creation of autonomous communities by formerly enslaved people) against colonial slave economies. Vibrant land struggles in the twentieth century included southern African countries' postcolonial land reform, such as the agronomic study of Amilcar Cabral in Guinea Bissau and Cape Verde,[1] La Via Campesina's founding in 1993 and the wider food sovereignty movement. More recent inspiration includes Vandana Shiva and peasant seed savers, the Movimento dos

Trabalhadores Rurais Sem Terra (landless rural workers in Brazil) and reparative justice movements centring land (including #Land-Back). As an inspiration in solidarity, it is also essential to recognise the enduring land-based struggle of agrarian Palestinians to continue ancient farming and ecological practices under increasing occupation, persecution and greenwashing by successive Israeli settler-colonial forces.

The 2019 report *Land for the Many*[2] revealed policies and everyday practices in the land system that were designed to keep the working class, Black people and other oppressed communities off of most land in Britain. This included the state's, aristocracy's and monarchy's ownership of land, trespass laws and systematic exclusion from access to most land in Britain. Land justice and regenerative agriculture movements in Britain are making connections between the inherited British estates of individuals such as MP Richard Grosvenor Plunkett-Ernle-Erle-Drax and their ancestors' engagement in plantation economies in countries such as Barbados, for example. These movements are resisting systematic exclusion across the world and its effects on farming and well-being, as well as repairing the mistreatment of the land itself. Examples include the use of vast swathes of land to imprison disproportionately Black and Brown peoples; racialised health inequalities resulting from being forced into built environments; and the policing of borders through deportation, detention and the hostile environment determining who can be on this land, who feels a sense of belonging here and who feels at risk of being removed. There is an ecosystem of struggle, resistance and liberation pushing through the cracks of the status quo.

Here, we focus on a particular element of land justice: access to land, particularly for food growing. From rural racism to the racist planning departments in town councils, access to land to grow food is often limited for BPOC in a number of ways, preventing access to work in horticulture/land-based work, access to growing foods that have ancestral and cultural significance, and access to fresh good quality fruit and veg. The last of these is especially significant given that many BPOC live in food insecurity (four times the national average).[3]

Cues have been taken from the increased articulation of land reparations for farming (as opposed to housing) by land and reparations campaigners such as Leah Penniman from Soul Fire Farm in upstate New York and the work of organisations such as Black Rootz and other BPOC-led food-growing projects in Britain, as well as calls for reparations from a range of groups including Stop the Maangamizi, climate justice campaigners and individuals reckoning with colonial generational wealth.

The work and organising principles of the Land In Our Names (LION) collective provide a lens through which to examine intersections of land and racial justice: the history of how access to land has become so racialised; the resistance strategies of BPOC to gain access, healing, reparations and belonging today; and the role of antiracist movements in the struggle for the creation of communities of support, survival and reparation inform our organising approach. Sharing stories of resilience from BPOC at the forefront of these intersections, together with a call for continued and expanded land reparations, the redistribution of land and financing and resourcing BPOC land projects, enables us to work towards building the BPOC community and improving and expanding intersectional food-growing movements, which are currently in their adolescence in Britain today.

Histories of Enclosure, Colonialism and Exploitation

> Revolution is based on land. Land is the basis of all independence.
> Land is the basis of freedom, justice, and equality.
> Malcolm X, 'Message to the Grassroots', 1963

The connections between land, capitalism, colonialism and racism are not always obvious because a tool of racial capitalism is to manufacture ignorance about history, especially among white people.[4]

In Britain, the current system of land ownership arrived with the Norman Conquest in 1066. A model of ownership was introduced whereby the aristocracy owned 50 per cent of the land by the time of the Domesday Book in 1086 – the first record of land ownership in this country.[5] Land was taken violently from the people who had previously lived upon it. This process continued across the centuries. From the twelfth century, landowners began putting up hedges and fences, influenced by ideas of efficiency in farming techniques. These informal enclosures were sanctioned by Parliament from 1604 onwards. Between 1604 and 1914 there were 5,200 enclosure bills, which fenced off one-fifth of England into private ownership. Enclosure forced more and more people off the rural lands which could meet their needs, away and into the cities. People's dependence on wage labour would instead be exploited from the late eighteenth century onwards to meet the needs of a capitalist industrialising economy.[6]

At the same time as enclosure was being formalised by Parliament, Britain's colonial expansion and establishment of the transatlantic slave trade were taking place. Profits generated from the violent exploitation and domination of subjects across the empire were being used to buy up land back in Britain. Even following the formal abolition of slavery by Britain in 1833, money from the Compensation Bill was paid by the British government to the owners of formerly enslaved people – and the debt borrowed by the state on money paid to slave owners' compensation was not fully repaid until 2015.[7] Money generated on the cotton plantations of the United States generated wealth back in Britain through the industrial revolution.[8] These cycles of enclosure, colonial expansion, participation in the slave trade and the profits it generated, even after abolition, shaped who could buy land in Britain, and access to the land became a matter of material resources as well as belonging.

From the early nineteenth century to the present day, there has been a shift in focus regarding who is allowed to enter this country, where they can go and what they can do: from the Aliens Act in 1905, which aimed to permanently restrict immigration into Britain, to the creation of detention centres from 1996 onwards and deportations highlighted through the Windrush scandal. Alongside this racialised policing of who is in and who is out, there are internal processes of policing and prisons that seek to determine who is allowed where and to do what.

Resistance and Struggle

Alongside these histories of dispossession, violence and domination are histories of land as a site of resistance and struggle. At every point along this timeline, outlined above, people resisted and tried to build alternatives. To name but a few of many examples: the Peasants Revolt of 1351; the Diggers taking up St Georges Hill in 1649; uprisings of the enslaved on plantations epitomised in the Haitian Revolution which lasted from 1791 to 1804, liberating the colony of Haiti; and the many independence movements that liberated colonised places across the world. Present-day movements follow in these lineages fighting for justice, from Black Lives Matter to abolitionist movements and No More Exclusions' campaign in education, as well as the struggle for tenants' rights and wider housing struggles.

Until recently there was limited dialogue in Britain about the intersections between land and racial justice, partly because much of the history outlined above is never discussed or taught in the mainstream conversation of this country. But the concept of land as a site of healing and struggle for Black and Brown communities is rapidly gaining traction. Land offers the possibility for reparation from historical legacies of colonial violence, the perpetration of the transatlantic slave trade and resulting injustices to this day.

LION emerged within these wider struggles. In its formative weeks, LION's co-founders ruminated over how to remedy the great wrongs inherent in exploiting people and land. As a variation of the popular migrant's retort coined by Ambalavaner Sivanandan, 'we are here because you were there', I, Josina, settled on 'our ancestors did not farm here [in Britain], but they farmed for here'.

Reinvigorating the British land justice movement and increasing the use of a reparative justice framework by land and food sovereignty initiatives were both central to LION's development, as well as increasing consciousness among BPOC in Britain around food growing, connecting to nature and climate and environmental activism. As with many recent joiners to the food-growing movements, LION's co-founders were 'driven by climate anxieties, and a sense that any home in our future lies in a better relationship with the land, spiritual ecologies and drawing on our budding knowledge of how to grow food'.[9]

Since 2019, LION has connected BPOC from formerly colonised countries, descendants of enslaved peoples and those whose global majority ancestors were integral to building the wealth of Britain. We have been providing a unique collective perspective as diaspora BPOC in Britain – the heart of empire. LION aims to build momentum for a land and food justice movement that seeks to transform systems in ways that both repair the past and create futures that are just for all. Our events provide an opportunity to celebrate and feel joy together, combined with an opportunity for sharing difficulties faced and painful experiences, which include reckoning with the niche challenges of rural life, land-based or farming activities or participating in outdoor leisure. Our work exists in a grassroots ecosystem that accumulates and shares knowledge on land ownership, colonial botany, food production and the relationship to the more than human living world.

The Experiences of BPOC Landworkers and Food Growers

LION completed two research projects with partner organisations aimed at identifying barriers to entry into the commercial food system in London and what can be done to enable new farming entrants to gain access to land. These two reports are *Rootz into Food Growing* (RIFG) and *Jumping Fences* respectively.

Both reports included coverage of how BPOC landworkers and food growers are resisting, healing and transforming the status quo. Describing the challenges provides context for the organising principles and responsive strategies adopted by both LION and BPOC food growers.

Racism

Many BPOC landworkers experience racism in the form of macro and micro aggressions as well as structural racism. One participant, feeling isolated and experiencing racism, spoke of the need for a 'thick skin' attending agricultural college. They knew few other Black farmers but were unable to talk with anyone in a similar situation. Several interviewees described this 'thick skin' as a personal survival strategy. The Jumping Fences author personally struggled with this coping strategy, reflecting that, 'by encouraging BPOC to develop a thicker skin, and stronger resilience to microaggression, overt racism and systemic racism, we give a licence for racism to continue'.

Isolation

Interviewees often reported experiencing isolation. For some, the isolation presented as a lack of support and a consequent perception of being less competent in their industries. Several interviewees voiced a struggle to access land, markets to sell, training and support networks.

Labour conditions

Some interviewees experienced burnout. Others suffered from the physical consequences of harmful agricultural practices negatively impacting on their health and well-being. Many commented on the voluntary/low-paid labour that is often expected for new entrants in food-growing spaces.

Land injustice

One participant in the *Jumping Fences* report observed the inherent injustice in the land system: 'Your average white farmer is quite privileged, usually male, often a landowner or even if he's a working-class farmer, he's going to have a historic tenancy, and he is going to get access to land because he's in that community. It is so much harder for people of colour to break into farming'.

Despite the many challenges associated with land inequalities, and the need to grapple with the harms of enslavement, colonialism and empire, landless BPOC land stewards feel powerful, with a shared sense of purpose, when so much is wrong in the world; creating opportunities to feed communities, acting on a felt responsibility to steward land in replenishing ways and encouraging holistic activities related to food, land and farming is deeply healing and vital to building the power of a movement for land and racial justice in Britain.

The Principles and Strategies

Two of LION's organising principles are *celebration* and *joy*: celebrating BPOC working the land and developing a relationship with the land; celebrating multiple food ways and lineages of growing, farming and tending the land; celebrating spiritual ecologies and the survival, presence and thriving of BPOC communities in a society that works constantly for the opposite.

> I ended up a farmer in the UK because I missed something that I grew up eating in Zimbabwe ... The only way to enjoy the food that I grew up eating is to grow it myself. And actually I didn't grow it because I wanted to sell it. I started growing because I wanted to enjoy the food with my family.[10] (RIFG)

Food has a considerable power to keep communities' connection with homelands and cultures alive. Interviewees had deep place-based connections to growing and many related to heritage through food.

The passion all growers and farmers had for what they did was reminiscent of Poet Toi Derricotte's line, 'joy is an act of resistance'. Joy could be found in many aspects of land-based learning, alongside building power and organising in land-based work and agricultural spaces. One interviewee said: 'I think it just changed my entire life, and reorientated my value system and what I chose to do with my time, what I spent my money on, what I spent my emotional energy on, completely shifted'.

The centring principles of *healing* and *repair* in the work of LION have been of vital importance to the way the collective has gone about its work. It has allowed spaces to be created on the land for BPOC to gather, sharing healing and restorative practices in community spaces, stories of ancestral knowledge and lineages of growing practices, and advice on saving seed and practising herbal medicine.

A key finding from the *Jumping Fences* report was that 'land work is *a source of healing* for racialised people'. Similarly, a RIFG interviewer spoke of 'hav[ing] faith ... a belief in the land taking care of us' despite the hardship experienced. For racialised peoples, LION's studies suggest these deeper spiritual connections with land and cultivation could support recovery from the negative experiences of racism. As with many farmers and growers with diasporic African heritage, ancestral connection was central in how some interviewees viewed their work – and this throughline was in many ways what was healing. As one report said, 'healing and traditional African practices are becoming more important in her farming practice, and connecting with other BPOC has been important for this'.

Participants with previous employment in fields with harmful environmental impacts, such as mining or landscape gardening, expressed wider 'world healing' through land-based livelihoods. And many interviewees were motivated to use regenerative practices, counter the ecological crisis and address climate anxieties and environmental degradation. One flower farmer was strongly motivated to provide an alternative to the high ecological impacts inherent in conventional flower farming.

For LION, '*reparations are about redistributing resources* to Black people and people of colour and creating space for BPOC to heal and repair. Financial reparations help secure economic resilience by redistributing money and land. Reparations must also address ecological, emotional and physical repair as essential.' In the *Jumping Fences* report Terry writes: 'A reparative justice proposes restoring relations to the land through social, cultural and material rebalancing of resources from those that have benefited from historical forms of oppression such as the slave trade and colonial empire, towards those that have inherited suffering under such oppression.'[11] Many vibrant campaigns and organisations are increasing the power of movements calling for reparations, perhaps most famously the CARICOM[12] ten-point plan for reparatory justice, the social movements demanding reparations for slavery in the USA and the work of Stop the Maangamizi, Esther Stanford-Xosei and the Seeding Reparations campaign in Britain. The MAIA Group[13] and the Black Land and Spatial Justice Fund are explicitly connecting the *land*, *abolition* and *reparative* threads. Cradle Community also recently spoke to the intersections between abolition and the land justice movement.[14]

LION wants to foster a relationship with the land, challenging and addressing the harms of colonialism. This includes going beyond 'extractivism': the removal of large quantities of raw or natural materials primarily for export. Though the impact of extractivist economic models on biodiversity and the climate receives deserved criticism, there are few initiatives to address the historic land theft which extractivism requires to function, or to establish community land trusts and land grants for dispossessed groups. LION's organisers are reimagining the relationship between humans and the land, and want to repair the historic and ongoing dispossession of land, including common and public land, green spaces, land for play, rest and living, and so on.

LION is also keen to support reparative practices on and with the land. *Regenerative agroecology* is an approach to healing relationships with the land, as part of addressing the earth's degradation and the climate crisis. Plenty of popular farming and food-growing wisdom and practices originate or were appropriated from Afro-Indigenous knowledge passed down through millennia. LION tries to honour these sources and strives for mobilising a thriving, inclusive and radical ecosystem of BPOC landworkers and land and food justice actionists, with the hope that a more robust ecosystem encourages new people to enter land-based living. This is partly achieved by celebrating existing action and people from urban community gardens to farming in rural areas.

One of the main challenges within the current land system is that *access to land* is severely limited. According to Guy Shrubsole's book, *Who Owns England*, half of England is owned by fewer than 1 per cent of the population.[15] Access to land is limited by rising costs, making it prohibitively expensive to buy. Anti-trespass laws make land inaccessible to all but the landowner. On top of this, rural racism can create a felt sense (sometimes backed up by verbal and physical violence) that BPOC are not welcome in the countryside.

Kinder in Colour marked the 90th anniversary of the Kinder Scout mass trespass. This event tried to make visible and disrupt various barriers facing BPOC in the English countryside. While this event garnered a lot of attention in the national press,[16] and many of the people who attended celebrated the possibility of coming together and walking in the Peak District, whiteness dominated the experience of several BPOC who attended. From the white gaze of the media taking photos of rituals on the land to white people taking up space at what was supposed to be a BPOC-centred event, overcoming the domination of rural spaces even at an event specifically about this proved challenging. In 2023, BPOC-only spaces have been organised by Right to Roam and Peaks of Colour. There is still a lot of work to be done regarding mixed spaces that focus on the BPOC experience and the opportunity to benefit from transformative healing – work that white people need to do to be able to enter mixed spaces and not practise oppressive dynamics. Reflecting on this experience has pointed to a concept coined by the Civil Rights Movement organiser Bernice Johnson Reagon,[17] who said that in movements we need home spaces where we feel at ease and can heal and share experiences and prepare to go into coalition spaces which are maybe more challenging but where we can organise across difference and build the power we need. How we do this work is something the movements for land and racial justice are working on in Britain – we aren't there yet.

The two LION research projects sought to understand barriers to access for BPOC landworkers, outline strategies that are currently being deployed to meet and overcome these barriers, and make recommendations for change. Many barriers to access are named: from rural racism to the cost of land to appalling working conditions. As both reports argue, the entry, and staying power, of BPOC into land-based livelihoods is an act of resistance in itself. The creative use of small growing spaces and allotments by growers in cities, developing resistance and resilience strategies to microaggressions and rural racism in the countryside, and the development of Black-led land/growing projects to improve access were all named.

Transformation: 'Building the Just World to Come'

Repair and reparations for past harms are of vital importance and one of the ways reparations can be achieved is by improving access to land for BPOC communities. However, there is a need to go beyond access to land within the current paradigm, and on this we follow the work of Olufemi O. Taiwo, who describes the constructive view of reparation as 'a historically informed view of distributive justice, serving a larger and broader worldmaking project. Reparation, like the broader struggle for social justice, is concerned with building the just world to come.'[18] Taiwo's focus on how to distribute benefits and burdens in creating a more just world looks to the past to determine how to allocate this distribution. But he argues that there isn't a moment in the past we can return to: reparations is a future-oriented project and requires the transformation of our world.

The wider land justice movement calls for the transformation of land systems as a whole: the ways people relate to land, considerations of how land is stewarded for present and future generations, and the ways land is farmed. This transformation includes moving away from industrialised agriculture towards regenerative farming and agroecological practices. Where LION and other BPOC groups may differ from mainstream (white) land activists is the view that addressing colonialism's harmful impacts is necessary for collective liberation. That colonial-rooted impact manifests as a trauma separating people from the land and each other. Reparative justice alongside regenerative land practices are routes to healing traumatic separation. Creating spaces to address issues of land ownership, access and belonging can offer routes to repair. This means that racism must be addressed, particularly as it shows up in green and rural spaces and unequal access to resources, as well as the visioning of new ways we might all relate to the land, steward the land for future generations and heal the legacies of the past into the present.

Building Community

The work of LION is to build a community across BPOC food growers and landworkers in Britain. Community building as a core principle is vital to the struggle, survival and thriving of BPOC communities. Through community support, which can be shared, celebration and joy can be realised, healing and repair can take place and connections can be built that create change through sharing knowledge, organising and taking action together.

In the research it seemed that many people were keen to teach each other how to grow and farm, building communities of knowledge and skill sharing. There were many strong advocates for the land-based livelihoods they had adopted. One participant 'relish[ed] the opportunity to teach people about the unsustainability of the import/export models' in the current food system. Many participants had experience teaching young people, and some had plans to set up growing academies or work collectively to buy land or grow food at a larger scale. One person shared 'the community of food growers. … It's been a great experience. You see other people doing different things to you, it's always a chance to learn. What I found was great camaraderie.'

There is the potential for collective action to be a second-stage strategy for existing growers who experienced isolation and see value in working with a larger group to achieve our goals. Through these two projects, it was clear how much potential food-growing and farming projects have for achieving social justice aims on the land. Many projects had these values embedded within them. For *Jumping Fences*, the author noted a 'development of critical consciousness – individuals are motivated and acting towards bringing diversity and justice into the farming sector'.

Food-growing spaces are underused, considering their great potential to bring diverse groups together for a shared purpose. Growing projects led by racially marginalised people have the potential to be deeply inclusive with clear social justice aims. They can be, as they have been in many antiracist struggles across the globe, used as sites of community building and strategising.

LION also sits in a *wider ecosystem* of land justice and antiracist collectives, organisations and movements. There is a spectrum of approaches in this ecosystem, from the radical to corporate diversity initiatives. LION works to transform narratives around land in Britain alongside many BPOC-led outdoor leisure and nature connection campaigns and organisations, including Black Girl Hike, Muslim Hikers and People of Colour in Nature. These groups are tackling the disconnect from the earth and living ecosystems, alongside the resulting poor mental and physical health outcomes. Some of these organisations also have land and spatial justice in their stated goals and principles. Acknowledgement of LION's shared goals with these organisations and movements of which LION is a part also comes with critical reflexiveness on approaches that sometimes differ. Organisations such as Black Girls Camping might focus on mental health, care and the well-being nature can bring, alongside advice and supported access to outdoor spaces through their events. In a similar vein, the Misery Party collective has held events sharing foraging, herbalism and fauna wisdom as part of its work on sobriety, healing and mental health. Organisations such as Flock Together focus on specific study or connection with wildlife. Others are loud about specific injustices, such as the #FreeSiyanda campaign, or in addressing rural racism in specific regions during the 2020 Black Lives Matter uprisings. Others may engage with or seek recognition from elected representatives, or attempt to lobby for law or policy changes. LION's approach may differ most from that which tries to appeal to an imagined good, 'non-racist', white rural population.

All of us involved in this work must beware the co-option of 'diversity in nature' into NGO-ization or ad campaigns serving corporate sponsors. As with other struggles, avoiding such dilution is a perpetual task for antiracist organisations. LION's reflexiveness on strategy and what solidarity looks like in associated movements will help in developing the capacity to demand reparations and create the transformation of society to one that is rooted in justice.

Conclusions

There are long histories of racialised oppression in Britain and by Britain, often driven by a desire to own land, exploit it and exploit people in the name of profit generation. This has left legacies today that determine who can own land, who can access it, who can grow what food where, who feels a sense of belonging in this place – and who does not. LION, alongside others, have been calling to attention the interconnections between land and racial justice and building communities of BPOC farmers and food growers to develop structures of support and solidarity in the face of racism, isolation and injustice.

In this chapter we have explored the organising principles that LION holds front and centre: celebration and joy, healing, repair and reparation, access to land, transformation – building the just world to come, building community and building social movements. Within each of these organising principles we shared insights from two ground-shifting pieces of research: RIFG and *Jumping Fences*. These insights came through the experiences of BPOC food growers, farmers and landworkers working in Britain today and from the stories of how BPOC communities are resisting land and racial injustice.

LION's work builds and strengthens BPOC land-based communities, developing resilience and regenerative practices. It is our hope that relationships can be fortified across movements and antiracist organising, with a better world envisaged through continued and expanded land reparation, redistribution and support for BPOC land projects.

Our collective strength to bring into being the changes we envision includes a shared understanding of the role of land in collective liberation and uplifting the BPOC food growers, farmers and landworkers at the forefront of such changes.

4

Weaving Together Internationalism and Global Solidarity in Britain

A roundtable with Akram Salhab, Asad Rehman, Elif Sarican, Martina Rodriquez and Mohammed Elnaeim

Akram Salhab is a Palestinian organiser, writer and PhD student at Queen Mary University of London, writing on Palestinian anti-colonial history. He has worked on numerous cross-community, migrant campaigns in Britain, and was previously the lead organiser of an initiative to reactivate the Palestinian Liberation Organisation through elections inclusive of all Palestinian communities around the world. He holds degrees in politics from the universities of Leeds and Oxford.

Asad Rehman is the executive director of War on Want, where he organises to put an end to poverty and injustice. Prior to that, he was the head of international climate at Friends of the Earth. Rehman has over 25 years of experience in the non-government and charity sector. He has served on the boards of Amnesty International UK, Friends of the Earth International, Global Justice Now and the Newham Monitoring Project.

Elif Sarican is a writer, curator and translator living in London. She is a long-term organiser in the Kurdish community in various areas including student, community and autonomous women's organising across Britain and Europe. She trained in social anthropology at the London School of Economics.

Martina Rodriguez is an Argentinian living in London and working as a political assistant at the Embassy of Argentina and a freelance writer. She is a founding member of the Feminist Assembly of Latin Americans, Ni Una Menos UK and the Argentina Solidarity Campaign. She has a BA in global politics and international relations from Birkbeck and is currently undertaking a postgraduate diploma in gender studies, diversity and subjectivity.

Mohammed Elnaiem is the director of the Decolonial Centre, a project of the Pluto Educational Trust, and a PhD candidate in sociology at the University of Cambridge. Mohammed is writing his dissertation on the relationship between capitalism, colonialism and patriarchy with the support of the Cambridge Political Economy Society.

* * *

In British politics, internationalism and global solidarity are often treated as niche issues: the idiosyncratic interest of certain politicians or organisations. The horrors of British imperialism, no matter their severity, are often confined to the margins of political debate, with occasional, short-term interest elicited only during particular crises. Israel's latest bombardment of Gaza, elections in Latin America, Kurdish resistance against ISIS, NATO withdrawal from Afghanistan, the Saudi war in Yemen – or similar events of global significance – momentarily flash across our TV screens and newspaper headlines, only to disappear once again, superseded by news of the latest Westminster scandal. Even news coverage of the looming environmental catastrophe lasts only as long as the most recent heatwave or protest.

These circumstances, however, are neither inevitable nor immutable. Indeed, British history is replete with examples of internationalist organising that have defined key moments in British history. The British public have often been severe critics of empire and slavery, and avid supporters of democracy movements on the European continent and beyond. During other periods of recent history, Britain was also host to exiles from around the world who turned the country, and London in particular, into a hub of anti-imperial organising and agitation across both the nineteenth and twentieth centuries.[1]

This spirit has been revived in the extraordinary mass protests on the streets of Britain in opposition to Israel's genocidal attack on Gaza, which has mobilised hundreds of thousands of people, seen renewed cross-community collaborations and brought questions of internationalism back to the forefront of British politics. What are the roots of these mobilisations, and how can the international sentiments underpinning them be strengthened ideologically and practically? How can mass dissent be organised to have a real impact in curtailing British imperialism and colonialism worldwide?

This roundtable seeks to contribute to the revival of internationalist traditions by bringing together the voices of key internationalist organisers in Britain to discuss the *terrain*, *principles* and *strategies* of internationalism today.[2] The roundtable has an overtly practical focus and aims to draw from organising experience to assess both the challenges of the present as well as to explore opportunities for future collaborative work.

Akram: I wanted to start by discussing internationalism and what it means at the present juncture in British politics. What does the term mean beyond a vague cosmopolitanism? How, as an organiser, is it connected to both your vision and practice of politics?

Elif: I came of age within a migrant community that saw itself both as a diaspora, concerned with the liberation struggle taking place back home, and as trying to embed itself here for future generations. The Kurdish community has always tried to integrate both these elements into its internationalist mobilising and organising. To understand internationalism and its meaning today, we need to start by learning about the different stages and histories of internationalist struggle that have come before us.

To me, internationalism means common struggle built on shared principles. This internationalism is woven into the very fabric of my political work and is part and parcel of our own struggle as the Kurdish people. As diaspora communities working across borders to maintain connections and sustain a movement, any meaningful and impactful work is inherently internationalist and involves manifold and deep connections at every level of our diaspora communities.

As such, Kurds see that it is impossible to envisage our own liberation outside a vision of international liberation, or conceive of a political struggle undertaken in isolation. That's why, for us, standing with the Palestinian people is not simply an expression of solidarity with a cause external to ours, but it is informed by the understanding that our liberation and freedom are intimately tied together, as the powers and systems that continue the oppression of our people are one and the same. The centrality of our belief in internationalism is also reflected in how the Kurdish movement has moved away from simply demanding Kurdish independence to a more democratic vision of society outside the confines of the nation-state system. The Kurdish movement calls instead for a moral political society built on the principles of radical democracy, ecology and women's liberation. So when we speak about liberating land that the Kurdish people inhabit, there is a vision – and inherently internationalist vision – of the society to be built on that land.

Martina: Internationalism is powerful because it implies coordination, action and organisation, not just between nations and movements but also peoples within Britain. We've seen this in the work we have done since 2017 in mobilising for Women's Strike, an effort at radicalising the demands of International Women's Day by undertaking an annual one-day strike on 8 March. In the process, we are building an internationalism that I have not seen before in terms of the degree of organisation and cross-communal, and the contact and connection between local and global issues and transnational networks of solidarity that have emerged from it.

So I agree that internationalism consists of approaching common struggles together, in our various contexts, while taking account of different realities. In the feminist setting in which I organise, this unity across difference is powered by the organising itself, and internationalism is a principle that informs so much of what we do – from defining our goals to mobilising, planning, strategising, organising events, creating content and thinking about and developing shared theories and ideologies. On an individual level I feel it means bringing a little bit of my country and our political struggles and connecting them to those taking place internationally.

This positive experience organising the Women's Strike contrasts with some of what I have seen in parts of the British left. I have often sensed something of a colonial mindset, and as migrants and Latin Americans we are often underestimated as a community, both politically and intellectually, and our traditions of political organising are not taken into account. This is very different from the incredible experiences we have had in building networks of feminist internationalism through Women's Strike and the sense of weaving together different experiences and traditions from around the world.

Mohammed: It is great to hear about Martina's experience, and it brings to mind something that has been in my thinking for some time, which is London as a meeting ground for so many different diaspora communities. During the height of the anti-colonial struggle in the mid-twentieth century, London facilitated many people from across different colonies coming together and enabled the building of a kind of common transnational anti-colonial programme. Over the past years there have been waves of protests that have somewhat helped revive this spirit of internationalism. This is most obvious in the huge support and turnout at protests for Kurdistan and Palestine, but there have also been significant mobilisations by Algerian, Argentinian, Chilean, Columbian, Haitian, Lebanese and Sudanese organisers, to name but a few.

It is important to recognise that these protests have not been happening spontaneously. Rather, they were organised by groups which have been doing this work for 15, 20 years, mostly without acknowledgement or any connection with the broader radical left. We need to recognise that the main repository of internationalism in Britain today is precisely such community groups, working behind the scenes for decades to manifest an internationalist politics.

Our main task at present is to build a broad political programme with these diasporic communities, both the older and the younger generations together, and connected to but not subsumed by parts of the political left. Although there are, of course, many different, sometimes conflicting political currents within these communities, I do think it is possible to come together around a shared set of principles that can inform and animate our collective struggle. Being here in this place together, many of us far from home, gives us a unique opportunity to build collective organising efforts based on both the liberatory currents in our individual traditions and our common heritage and experience of anti-colonial struggle.

Asad: Internationalism, for me, starts from an understanding of the global nature of the structures of oppression we face today. We are looking at a global system that, although manifesting itself differently in different places, is the same underlying system that requires a global response.

Today we are trying to weave together a movement that recognises that we need to be global in our own right and push back against the politics that says that the liberation and justice we seek can be achieved within an individual nation-state. Of course, the nation-state is an important point of intervention and a conduit for many oppressive global forces such as capital, racism and patriarchy, but we also know that none of these fights can be won within the confines of the nation-state.

Such an internationalism has been an integral part of progressive and revolutionary moments in history. You could go all the way back to the anti-slavery movement in Britain in the nineteenth century to see examples not just of a moralistic middle-class stance against slavery but also how working-class communities up and down the country mobilised in opposition to slavery, often drawing parallels with their own plight in the workhouses of Victorian Britain. We have seen many other moments where internationalism was the core of progressive politics in Britain.

As diaspora and exiled communities, we have direct experience of Britain's colonial foreign policy and are witnesses to the devastation it has wrought. So when we see British banks and corporations on the streets of London we don't see neutral logos, we see the machinations of extractivism, colonial oppression and environmental devastation that have shattered our people back home. This is the subjectivity and perspective we bring, and we seek to convey those realities into the British public space. For many of us there is an instinctive kinship of communities in struggles against the power structures we now live in and among.

Our political work, therefore, has two priorities: to bring together our communities in a common cause, finding shared stories and narratives and creating shared platforms for resistance; and trying to activate and reconnect movements and institutions that have increasingly turned inwards. The political work we undertake – organising, mobilising for key moments or providing political education – is directed at rebuilding international solidarity, and this term, solidarity, is to me at the core of our internationalism.

Akram: Through your organising work, what is your assessment of internationalism in Britain today, the success and weaknesses of existing modes of organising around it and the theoretical and conceptual gaps that exist? What are the challenges to creating the internationalist movements and politics we believe we need? We know, of course, of many structural barriers, from 'counter-terror' legislation and the hostile environment for migrants to harassment by the Charity Commission, defamation and much else. But what are the other considerations in terms of language or political action that you confront in your internationalist organising?

Elif: One of the biggest challenges I have encountered in organising in our community is the distance between the principled and strategic arguments for internationalism and the possibilities of integrating it into our everyday struggles. The situation back home is quite dire in many respects, and it keeps us busy fighting on so many fronts. Sometimes I feel the tension between the day-to-day struggles and the internationalist organising which we know to be essential but can sometimes be difficult to find the capacity for.

Another crucial point to highlight is the spirit we need to underpin this work. When reading the recollections of founding members of the Kurdish movement I noted that they invariably refer to themselves as romantics, connected to a radical and internationalist vision of freedom. For me this contrasts sharply with sections of the British left who are so focused on pragmatism at the expense of the political imagination as serious political and material work. Though there are historic political, social and economic reasons for this, and there are important events that happen in Britain – such as at the annual Durham Miners Gala – there is still a lack of a broader internationalist tradition and culture which is often regarded as outside a narrowly conceived understanding of 'political strategy'.

Martina: I agree that thinking about and organising around internationalism can be quite overwhelming, especially given the need to battle on all fronts simultaneously. This can be tough because we are often dealing with emergencies that we need to tackle in the moment – alongside what feels like equally urgent global crises.

The main question is how we can do both without losing capacity. To be sustainable, I think we need to build movements that can carry forwards this complicated work, and to do this we need to counter the fact that so many of us have become detached from any sense of community.

There are so many lessons and practical ways to build social consciousness. For example, in Argentina in 2015 there was effectively a femicide, with a woman being killed every 20 hours and alarming levels of opposition to feminism. But within two years we had built an international feminist movement that drew from our traditions of feminist struggle, politicised our own personal experiences of violence and linked our struggle with other emergent feminist movements, such as Women's Strike and the movement in Poland. This contributed to our growing sense of being part of a global feminist movement and allowed us to adopt an anti-imperialist politics by, for example, bringing Indigenous women to the forefront and connecting with the Kurdish women's movement.

We recognised that to build a movement we needed to be working with everybody, not just activists and academics, and that we needed to do this by focusing on the different manifestations of patriarchy. So we began striking for reproductive rights, striking for their recognition of labour, striking for the Indigenous women, always building around very concrete political actions, first locally and then trans-nationally and beginning from the people who were struggling in poverty, or those without political experience, connecting with all strata of society. We thought that to be genuinely internationalist our movement couldn't just be an elitist political movement. The fact that we were able to legalise abortion in Argentina, and to build a global mass movement with over 60 countries mostly from the Global South, is an incredible achievement.

One way we did this was through something called the National Women's Encounter – a yearly gathering of all the feminist groups in the country – who gather in a different province every year. It began with maybe 10,000 women and has now grown to about half a million women attending these conferences every year, expanding from the local to the global.

Asad: There was a time when our movements, by their very nature, were internationalist and expressed solidarity in common action. This was possible because there was a vision of the world that told you a story in which you could locate yourself. Even if you didn't know the details of each individual struggle, there was auto-matic support, for example, for the people of Kurdistan, Ireland, Palestine, South Africa or the Sandinistas in Nicaragua. You were the oppressed and had an automatic affinity with the oppressed, and understood in broad terms the machinations of gringo imperial-ism in Latin America, or British colonialism and imperialism in the Middle East. These structures, of course, have mutated with the con-nivance of our own domestic elites that have muddied the waters. We know that it might still be the same American or Western cor-porations pulling the strings, but now we are – ostensibly at least – fighting our own local elites, which changes the nature of people's material, day-to-day struggles, both at home and here in Britain. At this point I think that, as organisers, our work becomes – as we have said before – weaving together a new internationalism that considers what has happened in our recent history. I think we need to remem-ber that internationalism has always been something that needs to be constructed and maintained, not something that just drops from the sky on its own.

We've passed through cycles over recent years. The struggle against the wars in Iraq and Afghanistan 20 years ago were very important but ultimately quite narrowly focused, and the movement became overwhelmed by what was happening in Iraq. Around the same time there were efforts to build an anti-globalisation movement in opposition to the World Trade Organization, World Bank and International Monetary Fund (IMF). And 20 years before that, of course, we had the national liberation struggles, particularly in South Africa and of course today in Palestine. Put simply, our work is to recognise that we are in another epoch of struggle and we have to do the same thing that people who came before us did, which is to look at the lessons of the past, recognise the different context we are in and develop new tools and a new language to speak to and engage our communities.

Mohammed: I think we do certainly feel a sense of despondency and as though we've lost a common enemy that was the focus of the struggles of our predecessors. But we also need to be realistic and understand what the previous generations had to overcome in order to build a serious collective project. To give an example, the anti-apartheid movement in South Africa was riven with internal divisions that were responsible for keeping the apartheid project alive. The Third World liberation project had to consciously work to overcome this.

We need to address this in our political work, which will inevitably involve different types of political education, while remaining on the lookout for shared moments, demands and slogans around which we can start to build a common programme. Right-wing forces have managed to achieve this through an anti-establishment politics that touches on genuine grievances and connects them to a system and a global ideology through which to understand and analyse them. We need to aspire to build something equally comprehensive, flexible and ambitious.

One of the challenges here, and I will give Sudan as an example, is that many of our movements back home struggle to find a sustained organisational form through which they can maintain an internationalist politics long term. During the 2019 revolution in Sudan there were over 5,000 resistance committees in different neighbourhoods that organised the revolution and carried it through its different stages. The main opposition parties came to agreements with the Sudanese state and were part of what was billed as a 'democratic transition' or otherwise found seats at the table, which took them out of the ranks of the revolution. So I think we need to find a location for this internationalism within our movements, which, if it is not to be led by parties, needs to take place through bodies such as the resistance committees who are closer to the pulse of the people.

Akram: One thing that arises, when thinking about internationalism in Britain, is getting an understanding of the material circumstances in which we are working, who we are trying to mobilise and how. Today, a person's country of birth remains the greatest determinant of their income and I think people know this to a certain extent, which is why the reactionary discourse around migrants stealing jobs and collapsing the welfare state have proven so successful. There are very tangible material benefits which British society has gained from colonialism and slavery which I think British society is, at some level, aware of and keen to defend.

We can see this even in parts of the left that ostensibly support internationalist causes, such as the trade union movement, who often fund and support solidarity campaigns with Cuba, Palestine, Kurdistan and so forth, but whose membership includes a significant number of workers involved in building weapons that are then sold to the likes of Israel, Saudi Arabia and Turkey to commit atrocities. These unions will say that they exist to represent their members, not to determine the morality of the companies in which they work, but the contractions in their position are clear when a union rep expresses solidarity with Palestine one week and a week later heralds news job growth at BAE Systems as 'tremendously positive news for UK manufacturing'.

It is little use for us to simply condemn such positions (although we should), as it is structural and connected to the nature of British colonialism. We need to demand that our allies in trade unions not only speak about internationalism but organise on an internationalist basis in their workplaces and begin – in however small a way – to help dismantle imperialism by challenging an economy based on war and death and demand one based on life, ecology, human need and sustainability. The group Workers for a Free Palestine – established in response to the 2023 Palestinian trade union call to stop arming Israel – represents the beginnings of a rank-and-file movement demanding a principled trade union internationalist, in both word and deed.[3]

Akram: Among internationalists there is a tendency to look back at the Third Worldism of the mid-twentieth century as the heyday of a principled internationalism. How do you think we should relate to this period? What lessons do you think we can usefully draw from it? And which aspects do you think need to be rethought and reformulated for present conditions?

Mohammed: For me an important starting point is to realise that the previous generation of anti-colonial struggle were regarded as romantics. When the likes of C. L. R. James and George Padmore were saying in the 1930s that they wanted to advance the independence of Africa, everyone called them crazy and said that it wouldn't happen for at least another 100 years – but then we saw what happened only 25, 30 years later. It is important to emphasise how independence was achieved and how alliances and a common project were consciously and painstakingly built. This was not only on the basis of a shared enemy but a fuller sense of what liberation in a new world would look like, and that had to be shaped into a common Third World project.

One concern is that the necessary intergenerational learning from the Third Worldist moment to today is not taking place. Considerable parts of our migrant communities came to Britain as political exiles, and I know loads of young people whose parents were, or are still, involved in some kind of political movement. However, for most young people these movements are not something that second-generation migrants can participate in, and doors to them are often closed. When we were younger, some of us took it for granted that our parents were part of different political movements and we just weren't interested. Often parents themselves wouldn't know how to include us, or these movements began to collapse under the weight of internal disagreements. Whatever the cause, we haven't benefited from the rich traditions of the past or undertaken the analysis of our organising history that I think we need to.

Asad: I think we need to start by recognising that this history is a lived legacy and shapes what we say and do in the present in ways we often don't even realise. Many of the concepts, ideas and demands of the climate justice movement explicitly rely on the achievements of the non-aligned movement and Third Worldism.[4] I don't think you would have had the climate convention without the non-aligned movement or the idea of common but differentiated responsibility. You would never even have had the notion of 'sustainable development'. It was the non-aligned movement that said you cannot talk about the environment without talking about structures and injustices, as well as economic and social justice. So when the president of Barbados talks about the IMF and World Bank not being fit for purpose, she is drawing upon the non-aligned movement's advocacy for a new financial architecture.

More concretely, I do think there are practical lessons we can take from Third World movements: how they operated and built bonds of solidarity with others. For many it was a conscious political decision to build such alliances on the basis that their struggles were only going to be successful if they connected with other like-minded movements and peoples. This took place numerous times in Britain over the 1960s and 1970s, and even as recently as the 1980s, when the General Union of Palestinian Students organised with other Black student groups in the student movement.

Elif: The Kurdish freedom movement has a different experience of Third Worldism because it was founded at the end of the 1970s and flourished from the 1980s onwards, undergoing major ideological and organisational development over the period in which Third Worldism was in decline. One of the advantages of its relatively late appearance was that it developed – out of practical necessity – its own political centre, as it were, rather than relying on any one international connection or sponsoring state. I mean this both materially and ideologically in that it developed new political visions of liberation and was based on a synthesis of various ideologies (Third Worldism, communism, Kurdish nationalism, libertarian socialism, etc.) and its political experiences (organising alongside and in tension with the Turkish left, being trained by and fighting alongside the Palestinian Revolution). This, in part, explains the movement's resilience as well as why it doesn't have the same nostalgic perspective on the era of national liberation, given that it is still very much functioning and is arguably as strong as it has ever been.

This also changes how the movement approaches the question of intergenerational learning, which it sees not only in terms of learning lessons or principles that the youth then go away and practice, but as a process of mutual learning and common struggle. In this way, Kurdish youth can both benefit from past experiences as well as educating elders on the changing circumstances, politics and culture of today. That way we can draw from both the past and the present and take them into the future collectively.

Akram: For Palestinians and other struggles in a moment of organisational weakness, there is a danger to discrediting our revolutionary history. The postcolonial condition has, for good reason, produced a lot of reflection on the shortcomings of national liberation movements – their ideologies and institutions – that has often taken the form of identifying 'the cause of defeat' or post-mortems of failure. I am not saying that we haven't suffered setbacks, we clearly have, but our reading of history needs to be based on what was possible in the context in which these movements were organising, on a balance sheet of both what was lost and what was gained and on what we can learn from our revolutionary histories. We need to understand that the world would be in a much worse place had a whole generation not risen up and attempted, with significant success, to overturn centuries of colonial rule.

I see today that Palestinian formations are gaining a better understanding of the legacy of those who came before us and their role in laying the groundwork of Palestinian solidarity. It is easy to think that the protests for Palestine represent a spontaneous revulsion at Israel's genocide, but such mass mobilisations and awareness are only possible because of years of people's diplomacy, consciousness raising and alliance building in political parties, trade unions, faith institutions, students groups and twinning projects. This was led by Palestinian parties, individuals and unions who made inroads into what was a very hostile environment, where speaking about Palestine was virtually impossible. This was overcome through years of painstaking work, and we have much to learn from how this was achieved in order to appreciate that we are building on its legacy.

Akram: Finally, what would you say are the main takeaways from this discussion? What are the practical steps you think organisers need to undertake to realise the vision of internationalism we have described? What are the signs of hope that you perceive in the organising you see around you?

Asad: Overall I would say that I am an optimist, and I think that you need to be a romantic dreamer to believe that another world is eminently possible. I take real hope from moments such as one that took place in 2021 in support of Palestinian rights and the mass uprising of millions of people against Israel's 2023 genocide in Gaza. When you look at those attending marches and actions you can see that it isn't only 'the left' in attendance but also a huge number of young people, particularly those from Black, Brown and migrant backgrounds.

I think that this is significant as I often get the sense that first- and second-generation migrants behaved as though their presence in the diaspora in Britain was temporary and that they would eventually return home. For example, when the South Asian diaspora arrived in Britain it remained part of political formations such as the Indian Workers' Association, which drew heavily on Indian left political traditions and very much saw itself in this spirit. However, a generation or two later this is starting to change, and I think it is going to be fascinating for politics in this country when this new generation goes through schools and becomes part of the left. What changes can be brought about by large numbers of people from, for example, the Indian subcontinent, or of Kurdish, Palestinian or Somali descent – confident of their place in British society but carrying a new, uncompromising internationalism?

We are already beginning to see this – socially, politically and culturally – among young people who are aware that they are products of global capital, colonialism and imperialism. We should celebrate this as a victory, as there is now a generation growing up that does not question that our movement should be antiracist or should be fighting for women's liberation. Such principles appear to be imbibed to such a degree that it has become cultural – it is not even a political thing – which I think is incredible. And we see this new generation as the central organisers of Black Lives Matter and the environmental justice and Palestine solidarity movements, which is very promising for the future.

Mohammed: I think we need to build an assembly between different communities here in Britain that can act as a sort of confederation of democratic nations (a term which I borrow from the Kurdish movement): something that can bring us together, inform each other of our respective struggles and start to explore the building of common projects and areas of work. I've outlined a few examples of the prospective campaigns that could emerge from this: for example, around colonial apologies and reparations, militarism, climate justice and combating the criminalisation of our communities. This would form an important transnational way of not only working together and building power that would feed back into our individual struggles but also of sustaining and building an internationalist politics that goes beyond simply responding to crises back home and towards a global vision and political programme.

In terms of optimism, I would say we need only look at the international movements around the world today to see the incredible potential of what is being built. When I think about Chile, or Columbia, or the Indian farmer's movement for example, I feel very hopeful for the future. I think that a lot of pessimism derives simply from not looking up at what is happening in the world. I think we need to hold on to these movements and moments and keep policies and ideas alive until the politically impossible becomes the politically inevitable.

Elif: What inspires me is the Kurdish movement's development of a vision of a future society that directly informs organising in the present. For example, the Kurdish vision of women's liberation is embedded in their formations at home and in the diaspora that operate on the basis of a co-chair system in which leadership positions are shared equally between women and men, and decisions must be taken with the consent of both a democratic majority and a majority of women's structures. The connecting tissue between the vision and practice are the methodologies of struggle, in which political work is conceived less in terms of making society anew and more as giving society the tools by which it can remake and defend itself, and therefore be equipped to fight against the enemy.

We can see, for example, how the Rojava Revolution has begun to transform society based on the principles of radical democracy, ecology and women's liberation. These principles have become impactful through a political culture that reminds society of the democratic traditions that were destroyed by colonialism and incorporates these ideas into its songs, slogans and representations of society. We can also see how the slogans and messages of the Kurdish movement break through borders, such as the proliferation of the slogan *Jin, Jiyan, Azadî* – Woman, Life, Freedom – and its use during the uprising in East Kurdistan (north-west Iran) and Iran. The slogan was first chanted in Istanbul on 8 March 2006 and its keywords connect to the principles of the Kurdish movement: 'woman' reflects the belief in women's complete liberation and a society based on their full participation in all areas; 'life' connects to the principles of ecology (i.e. protecting an environmental that can sustain life); and 'freedom' as a radical, inclusive vision in which people make decisions for themselves.

These examples show how the revolutionary seed, once planted, can sprout in unexpected times and places, and spread and cross-fertilise struggles in many parts of the world.

Martina: How we approach the question of optimism and hope is, for me, connected to how we view the world and interpret our struggle. It can be easy to lose heart or feel down, especially if we assess our struggle as a continuum of failure and loss. But I am reminded of what an Indigenous woman who addressed our ecofeminist workshop the other day said, which was that we don't have any lost struggles, only learnings. I think we really need to absorb this and appreciate that we haven't lost anything so long as we continue the struggle and make sure that those past struggles live in us and in our actions.

Akram: Despite the barbarity of Israel's genocide, it is impossible to see the mass mobilisations for Palestine and not feel some sense of hope. It is clear, as Asad said, that a new generation is not only getting involved but taking the reins in conceiving of new radical actions and forms of solidarity, which take the fight for Palestine and internationalism not only into the streets but also into institutions: universities, schools, trade unions and workplaces.

Every single attempt by the British state to dampen people's outrage at the injustice in Palestine, or to curtail their expressions of love for our cause and our people, have utterly failed. Seeking to ban the Palestinian flag, solidarity marches or the chanting of certain slogans has had the opposite effect, igniting instead an outpouring of defiant solidarity at every level of society. I think people are responding both with a sense of empathy for Palestinians and the savagery, death and destruction they witness them living through and to their extraordinary – almost unbelievable – courage, steadfastness and resistance. It is clear to the world that the Palestinian people will never surrender, and this inevitably inspires them to want to match this heroism in their own lives.

All these actions and gestures are a beautiful light in the midst of the horror, and they call on us to redouble our internationalist work and consolidate the alliances, institutions and movements that can prevent such a genocide from ever recurring.

5
Solidarity Knows No Borders

Migrants Organise

As the crises of racial capitalism escalate, the ruling class in Britain have united in blaming migrants for the country's economic, social and political problems. The politics of the far right sits squarely in government, using migrants arriving by dinghy across the Channel as a distraction from the harsh realities of capitalism: from climate and ecological collapse to the continuous funding of imperial wars and genocides abroad, and the fact that most people in Britain are struggling to afford necessities such as rent, heating, childcare or more than basic groceries. The government's actions embolden fascists, who increasingly mobilise to physically threaten and intimidate people seeking safety in Britain who are housed in 'asylum hotels', and street attacks on racialised people are on the rise.

Simultaneously, the government is spending increasingly vast sums of money on cruel and brutal technologies to strengthen the border. This ranges from electronically tagging migrants, threatening wave machines to push back small boats in the Channel, imprisoning people on barges, trying to deport them to Rwanda, driving up visa fees and income requirements amid a cost-of-living crisis and escalating the number of immigration raids on workplaces, to name but a few. As musician and antiracist organiser Awate has pointed out, 'go back to Africa' is no longer a racist slur hurled at Black and Brown children in playgrounds: it is now government-mandated policy, with the Rwanda deportation plan the first step in a system in which people are forcibly kidnapped by the state and essentially disappeared.[1]

As migrant organisers working to end hostile border controls in Britain (and beyond), we must articulate and practise principled connections between antiracist and migrant justice organising, which have, over the last few decades, become more fractured, separated and siloed. We see the two as inseparable and as part of the same demand against racial capitalism. In this chapter, we affirm why organising against borders and in solidarity with people who move across them must be a fundamental part of any antiracist movement, and set out how we might start building 'an anti-racism fit for these anti-immigrant times'.[2]

We Are Here Because You Were There

People move. We always have done and always will: for love, for work, for family, because we were forced to by repressive state forces or the impacts of climate and ecological collapse, or for wanting something better and imagining a new life could be possible elsewhere. While migration is a fundamental part of human existence, borders have not always existed and are relatively new in their current formation. For many of us at Migrants Organise, this is deeply and personally understood. We or our parents, or grandparents, were alive at the moment when imperial and colonial forces carved up our homelands and erected new borders, often literally overnight, separating us from places we also knew as home, from family, neighbours, colleagues and classmates, with devastating consequences. It is the reason that many of us in Britain are involved in this work today.

Borders are not natural or necessary but are historically contingent regimes continually reproduced through a number of different processes, ordering populations as desirable or undesirable. Over the past three decades the reach and power of border controls have penetrated every area of life through the hostile environment immigration system. As Gracie Mae Bradley and Luke de Noronha put it, borders 'follow people around, excluding them in various ways at different times', thus producing the precarity and disposability that characterises the migrant condition – infringing on our ability not just to move territorially, but to work, love, see a doctor, drive a car, open a bank account, access benefits or any other forms of state support.³ We know that this thing called the 'border' is messy, not simply a line on a map but also a continuous process.

Borders do not exist for everyone in the same way: they discriminate. For the world's rich, borders are a minor inconvenience when travelling. Visas are afforded and obtained fairly easily, and freedom of movement or freedom to stay is barely curtailed. But for the global majority, borders are a hostile, immovable and inescapable feature used to criminalise, dispossess and expel.

We can directly trace the British state's immigration and asylum systems from the expansion and decline of the British empire and the transition from colonialism to modern day 'globalisation' (or neoliberal imperialism). We can understand the development of borders and border policy, as well as the generation of so-called border crises, as fluctuating in response to capital's need for labour: kidnapping enslaved peoples across continents in service of colonial wealth, population transfers across empire, the free movement of cheap and easily exploitable workers across Europe. Sivanandan captured the essence of the experience and politics of this history of immigration when he said, 'colonialism and immigration are part of the same continuum – we are here because you were there', following it with, 'globalisation and immigration are part of the same continuum. We are here because you *are* there.'⁴

Tracing this history into the present reminds us that 'immigration' cannot be defined as a 'domestic problem', but rather that 'borders between nation states perpetuate hierarchies made by colonialism'.⁵ Migration forces are global in scope and connected deeply to enduring processes of colonialism and imperialism. Therefore, organising for migrant justice in Britain requires us to be internationalists: invested in a project that is not about just transforming the conditions at home or confined by our nation-state but about transforming the world. We must not only be attentive to the freedom and dignity of people who move but also to their reasons for moving in the first place, which describe everything from climate and ecological collapse driven by the capitalist exploitation of land, people and resources, to wars driven by tensions and inflamed by empire or imperial forces. In being pro-migrant and pro-refugee, we must be anti-imperialist and anti-colonialist.

Thinking through the history of Britain's border regime requires us to think more deeply about the role of race and racism than that offered in much of today's mainstream debates. If racism is about 'discrimination' and 'hate crimes', rather than the structures that construct and maintain racial hierarchies, the connection between migration, borders and racism becomes obscured. But when we understand racism as a structure that is concerned with exclusion – that is, demarcating certain people as 'others' and 'outsiders' who are excluded from particular spaces or from having particular legal rights – then we can see how borders fundamentally produce racial distinctions and hierarchies. Racial capitalism requires boundaries to be constructed between 'super-exploited workers in the Global South, unfree migrant workers, and "free" citizen-workers', and to do so requires the construction of racial hierarchies and racism in order to normalise and administer these differentiations.[6]

It is not a coincidence that in Britain, the Home Office oversees the functions of the British state which (re)produce many of the major disciplining forces of racial capitalism: policing and the criminal justice system, immigration, counter-terrorism and drugs policy. Borders are by no means the only way that racial capitalism constructs race – many of the other chapters in this book explore the different ways in which antiracist organising responds to different manifestations of the construction of race and racism. But as antiracists and internationalists, it is important that we understand the ways borders play a major historical and continuing role in shaping the contours of global structures of racism. This connects the importance of struggles at an international level with the tools and technologies of racism at home.

Our analysis is that Britain's immigration system is not broken, but that it is hostile by design. The racism, dehumanisation and injustice experienced by migrants and racialised communities is not a failure of the system, it is the system. We work towards structural change that goes beyond reforms to the current white supremacist capitalist state and aims at something much bolder: at the abolition of borders and nation states, dreaming of a world based on our collective liberation and the flourishing of all life on earth.

In this context, then, what are the principles that guide us in how we organise as antiracists dreaming of a world where people have the right to stay and the right to move?

People Power

The task of organising against borders and for migrant justice may seem daunting, but we start with why we are invested in this fight: our people. We are moved to action by and because of our people and the power and strength that we have. We are involved in organising, which works alongside campaigning (aimed at individual policy change) and mobilisation (engaging people for a single action) to build long-term mass power from the bottom up. We are interested in organising because it seeks not just to secure an individual demand but a substantial and long-term redistribution of power. Building our power is a process and it takes time. In the face of relentless dehumanisation and scapegoating, we always return to the humanity of and love for our people.

In organising, we define power as the ability to act. There are many other forms of power, such as financial freedom, status and connections, an army or a political position. Most of us and our people do not have this kind of power. Instead, we recognise that our power comes from us – that if enough of us work together, we can change things for the better through 'relational power'. We are organised when we are in a relationship with each other: when we trust each other, see and value each other's humanity and can count on each other. We build trust so that we can identify problems in our communities, connecting them to historical and structural issues and injustices. Organised relational power is also about identifying values and spaces to co-design alternatives to oppressive systems and structures and take actions to make a change.

We can look to the Justice for Simba campaign as an example of building people power. Simbarashe Mujakachi – a young Zimbabwean man from Sheffield who dreamed of being a fitness instructor – needed NHS treatment for his blood-clotting condition. He went to his GP, and was referred for specialist treatment, but quickly started getting bills from the NHS, sometimes several thousands of pounds at a time. At the time, Simba's application for asylum had been refused and he was preparing a 'fresh claim'. The Home Office had separated his family, and due to the hostile immigration system, he was not allowed to work or study. He received a tiny allowance from the government to live on until that stopped too, and he relied on family and friends for support. He received phone calls from his hospital before operations he needed, and was told he had to pay hundreds of pounds upfront or else he wouldn't get treatment – so he stopped getting the care he needed. Just days before his thirtieth birthday in 2019, he had a haemorrhagic stroke and was rushed to hospital to receive life-saving brain surgery. When Simba woke up, paralysed on his left-side, the hospital's finance team presented him with a bill for £93,000 and told him that this debt could impact any future immigration application he made.

Simba turned to organising. His dad, Victor, met one of our organisers at an event, and together they started to organise, bringing family members and close friends (some who had been involved in Victor's anti-deportation campaign the year before) into contact with one another, and we formed the Justice for Simba campaign. It was built with and alongside the Patients Not Passports (PNP) campaign: a national campaign forged through the collective organising of healthcare workers and patients for universal health care and against borders in public services.[7] This partnership work emerged through relationships with Docs Not Cops, Medact and Migrants Organise. The resources, networks and experience of those involved in PNP directly fed into Simba's campaign and provided infrastructure for the campaign to grow in power and reach a much wider audience. We talked with antiracist organisers with many years of experience building individual and family justice campaigns to learn how to stop campaigns being co-opted or delegitimised by the state and how to connect 'cases into issues, issues into causes, and causes into a movement', and we worked with Simba to build a platform to talk both about his own experience and how it connected to the wider system of bordering and racism.[8]

Through the campaign, we built relational power across different sectors in Sheffield: with the football team Simba once played in, with the healthcare workers who provided his care and with community campaigners who had deep knowledge of the council housing priority ballot, among others. We located an immigration lawyer to help with Simba's case, a team to turn up to Simba's housing meetings with the council and a group of health workers who raised Simba's story with their colleagues at the hospital and became involved in the campaign. The health workers, organising with Medact Sheffield and PNP, reached out to local power holders and brought all four members of Parliament in Sheffield on board with the demands of the campaign to end the policy of charging migrants for their NHS treatment and sharing patient information with border enforcement. Through this process of slow, relational organising over more than three years, the campaign won support from people with positional power to end hostile environment border policies, including Olivia Blake MP, who shared Simba's story in Parliament during Black History Month, connecting the Windrush scandal and the ongoing deportation of Black British people with Sheffield's historic connections to the slave trade and to Simba's struggle against the hostile environment.

In January 2022, Simba won his campaign – he was granted refugee status, and soon after the hospital confirmed that they would wipe his entire NHS debt. Simba's campaign was a crucial part of the work growing the network of hundreds of healthcare workers with radical anti-border politics organising in their hospitals through the PNP campaign. It helped demonstrate that Simba's story did not exist in isolation but was part of a deliberate government policy of exclusion, racialisation and violence. These health workers continue to organise in their workplaces against border controls in health care, and have connected NHS charging with wider struggles against privatisation and the creation of a system which can charge those deemed as 'undeserving' for their health care. Simba went on to connect with others who had been subject to NHS charges but had been too scared to speak out, and who have since started publicly campaigning.[9] At the heart of this work is the fundamental belief in our people: that each of us has power, and when we work together, we can enact change.

Solidarity, Not Charity

Solidarity, not charity, is another core principle at the centre of our organising. This means emphasising dignity and mutuality and recognising that our collective liberation is bound together. We recognise that people cannot organise unless we can physically survive. We cannot ignore people's material needs or refuse to work with them: starting with where our people are at often means starting here.

Britain's immigration system is designed to drive people into precarious, exploitable and degrading situations, where access to basic services (such as housing, health care, work, legal support and education) is restricted and criminalised. Under Britain's border regime, the government will not look after us, and so we must look out for each other. This is why we build mutual aid networks and cultivate communities of care who can work together to provide the things that we all need to flourish. SOAS Detainee Support puts it best: 'When we act from solidarity, we foreground the views and needs of those who are directly harmed by our immigration system. When we organise in opposition to hierarchies, we can build the power and networks needed to dismantle the racist and oppressive immigration system for good.'[10]

We do not do this work because we want to 'save' people who are framed as victims of a 'broken' immigration system. As such, our approach stands in stark contrast to large sections of the professionalised migration and refugee 'sector'. In the charitable framework, people on the move are deserving of our help because they are help-less victims, a narrative that denies agency or any meaningful voice. Charities encourage people (citizens) to donate money, without meaningfully attempting to challenge the conditions that give rise to hostile border policies in the first place.

The Migrants Organise Housing Collective is a group of Migrants Organise members and friends, all of whom have precarious immigration status. The group meets to organise for better living conditions in housing, and it is currently focused on building power to target private companies, such as Clearsprings Ltd, who profit from keeping people in degrading 'detention' hotels and deteriorat-ing multi-occupancy housing. The Housing Collective embodies the practice of solidarity not charity by sharing learnings of sur-vival strategies and taking action to improve material conditions for themselves and their friends. They deliberately take time to build relationships with each member of the group and to create spaces where people can openly share how they are feeling, share hot drinks and food, and make time for collective joy.

By connecting with others facing similar issues and finding cre-ative ways to take action, the Housing Collective is organising for a long-term redistribution of power, and it is able to make material differences to their own lives by going beyond a model that relies on charities reactively stepping in to help 'solve' their problems. When thinking critically about how this organising can build the world we want to see, the Housing Collective acknowledges that this way of organising is time intensive and may not amount to system trans-formation tomorrow, but it requires all of us to play an active role in our communities. It requires us to practise hope, which Mariam Kaba set out as: 'taking action is a practice of hope ... To transform the conditions of our oppression(s), we can only do what we can today, where we are, in the best way we know. We can only survive together.'[11] And surviving together means discovering that we have the solutions to the oppression facing our communities, and that we will be the only ones to save us. As one of the members of the Housing Collective, Nanou, said: 'this shows that when we organise together, we can build the world we want to live in, brick by brick: a world where we have dignity and justice. But we should not have to fight for the bare minimum.'[12]

Communities of Resistance

One of the most important tools that we have against the government's attempts to divide and rule is our ability to build connections and coalitions as people who are intentionally separated and divided from each other. The Solidarity Knows No Borders (SKNB) community of resistance organises within and across different migrant communities: people with different immigration statuses, people who have been here for different lengths of time, people organising in different locations and with different targets.

Born to address the desperate need for a strong migrant-led movement for justice, the SKNB community unifies organisations across Britain: migrant and refugee groups, faith organisations, trade unions, charities and many other associations and individuals committed to migrant justice in a common fight that recognises the systemic nature of the racism we are fighting against. Not everybody defines themselves as a border abolitionist, nor is everybody working towards the same goals. The strength of the movement is that different organisations, groups and individuals are resisting many different facets and aspects of the hostile immigration system, in the process building new systems of care and imagining a better future. This is the work of movement building: bringing together local, regional and sectional interests and campaigns into a broader alliance with greater ability to bring about change. Alone, groups and campaigns are weak, but together we can acquire sufficient strength to seriously challenge the structures that we are confronting.

SKNB members aim to 'do no harm' to each other and each other's aims, taking our lead from those who are or have been subject to immigration controls. Doing so requires us to be attentive to each other's needs and interests, to understand struggles that are different from our own and to not limit or restrict the actions and activities of different groups and organisations with whom we work. Importantly, this means recognising that there are tactics where we may disagree. For those working in non-governmental organisations, mainstream advocacy organisations or within the legal systems, this means not denouncing groups who take a more radical approach – whether that be through direct action or more radical demands – or punching leftwards in an attempt to appeal to an imagined 'centre ground'. For some grassroots groups, it means not denigrating the importance of institutional approaches when it comes to supporting our people in the here and now, or outright rejecting others' tactics in pursuit of political purity. Being able to work together and hold each other accountable is particularly important when the wider political terrain is so hostile and the broad goals of the movement are to limit the harms and resist the daily violence that aims to exhaust and divide us.

For example, the government's plan to send an inaugural flight of people seeking asylum to Rwanda was grounded in June 2022 because of a variety of different tactics from individuals, groups and organisations with different approaches, ideologies and political inclinations. People detained at Brook House removal centre and threatened with removal went on hunger strike; a collective of activists, under the banner of Stop Deportations, took direct action to physically prevent a coach from leaving Colnbrook removal centre, which delayed the flight taking off, while legal teams launched challenges which went all the way to the European Courts at record-breaking speed to get people off the plane; organisations such as Freedom From Torture and others launched popular public campaigns against the private companies who were providing charter flights and were forced to back out of the plan (building on successful campaigning of those involved in the Stop TUI campaign some months prior); the SKNB network held a week of action in the week the flight was due to take off, holding protests outside Home Office buildings in cities across the country, and much more.[13] The work for antiracist organisers involves reflecting on the strengths of multidisciplinary approaches in service of the long term and understanding how we move beyond firefighting in the face of relentless attacks.[14] This means recognising the need to practically support people on the basis of solidarity not charity, building people power and unity, and developing connected, caring communities of resistance.

Tools for Pragmatic Border Abolitionists

In the process of organising against racism and against all the structures that uphold racial capitalism, we try to build new practices of care and support for our communities, even as we try to tear down the structures that don't work for us. As Ruth Wilson Gilmore says of the work of abolition, it 'is about presence, not absence. It's about building life-affirming institutions.'[15] In our organising, we are constantly evaluating and re-evaluating our targets, demands and strategy to ensure they are consistent with the world we want to win. With each change in the political landscape, we must develop the tools to assess reforms, demands and targets against the goalpost of total liberation, as opposed to the goalposts we are told we must settle for.

While campaigns to address the immediate and material needs of our people in our communities are vitally important, we have learned that attempts to address them without addressing the structurally hostile environment border system and racial capitalism are rarely successful and can backfire. Instead, we work at developing grassroots organising strategies that are attentive to the here and now, while remaining in service of a vision of total liberation. These strategies are designed to undermine and limit the coercive and oppressive state practices of bordering in the world we currently live in, while building our power to get to the world we want to win. These are sometimes referred to as 'non-reformist reforms', which are 'the material changes that further open the way to a world without borders'.[16]

An example of this is the way the Abolish Reporting campaign navigated the Home Office's decision to introduce telephone reporting conditions to more people. Abolish Reporting is a national campaign calling for a world built on principles of care, not surveillance. Anyone waiting for a final decision on their application to live in the UK can be required to regularly travel to 'report' at an Immigration Reporting Centre. Every appointment carries the risk of being randomly taken to a detention centre and threatened with deportation. In 2020 and 2021, as many of our members were being forced to report during the coronavirus pandemic, we launched the Abolish Reporting campaign with These Walls Must Fall (a network of refugee and migrant campaigners working for the end to detention) to call for an end to reporting conditions – full stop. The campaign came out of a collective of our members who started to speak out against the injustice of reporting, the burden and restrictions it placed on their lives and the huge waste of resources that went into this system of keeping people under constant state surveillance.[17]

In 2022, when the Home Office announced that telephone reporting would be the new standard method of reporting, instead of in-person reporting, we saw first hand the importance of pushing for structural change instead of piecemeal reforms alone. Because our campaign vision and demands were explicitly focused on demanding an end to all immigration reporting for all people, we were able to recognise the limitations and dangers of the policy change to telephone reporting.

We asked ourselves questions: is this change reducing the power of the state to surveil and control people? Does it help more people get free together, or does it instead divide us and pit one person's freedom against another's? Will this change be used to justify new modes of control and surveillance or to reduce them? As organisers, we recognised that, if implemented properly, telephone reporting could help reduce the material, physical and psychological burden of immigration bail on people's lives. It also helped demonstrate that change was possible: for a long time, in-person reporting was treated as a fixed status quo. But we saw even the Home Office admitting that in-person reporting was unnecessary.

If we were not actively working for structural change, perhaps this would be enough. But we found it important to highlight other considerations: some categories of people would still be asked to report in person. Telephone reporting itself could be distressing and burdensome, for example, for the many migrants facing destitution who may not be able to afford a phone or credit. There was also the fact that, alongside the move to telephone reporting, the Home Office was rolling out other forms of surveillance for reporting, such as GPS ankle-tags. These considerations made it important for the campaign to approach the policy change with caution. After all, we were a campaign to abolish reporting, not make reporting slightly less inconvenient for some people.

Unfortunately, since 2022, the Home Office has ramped up its attempts to surveil and control migrants through immigration reporting, especially through GPS tracking. But, as a group of people dedicated to changing the system of the hostile environment and not simply making it slightly less hostile, we were ready to respond and fight back. We have built a collective of people who take action together, developed our politics and understanding together, and created the tools and infrastructure to make decisions based on the world that we want to win.

Building a World beyond Borders

Borders are not a natural fact of life but have been in the making for centuries to serve racial capitalism. Abolishing borders is as much about getting rid of unjust systems as it is about building new ones that embody the values we want to take into the new world: dignity, abundance and freedom for all. From Liverpool to Coventry, Folkestone to Sheffield, London to Hastings, migrant-led groups, together with community associations, antiracist organisations, renters' unions, climate groups, healthcare workers and many more, are joining together to stand up to the increasingly authoritarian forces that seek to divide us. In the face of relentless attacks, we see beauty in the solidarity and commonality in our struggle.

Our experiences of organising for migrant justice is that this work is hard: in the current political landscape, it feels like we are losing more than we win, and many of our people face profound harms and violence. In this context, none of our victories are small or insignificant, and much of the task at hand is making visible the fact that we do have power – that when we are organised and when we work together, we can and do win.

Building power in our communities means starting where you are and with the people around you, creating networks of care and support, collective learning and space to imagine a world without borders and new ways of living together. Only together can we bring them to life. If you are not already organising and would like to find out what is already going on near you and how to join, visit the SKNB website: www.sknb.org. If you want to start organising, find us at Migrants Organise: www.migrantsogranise.org.

We are indebted to our members, to the people we are in struggle with and to the many thinkers, writers and organisers who have shaped our work. The arguments we make here offer lessons from our experiences of organising but are by no means exhaustive, nor a final product. We hope that this book will spark questions and conversations, and contribute to our collective learning in the pursuit of getting free together.

6

Time Travelling: Organising for Antiracist Futures

Healing Justice London

The Future is Ancestral.

Kaxinawá/Huni Kuin proverb

The thing is if we [are] talking about collective liberation, we are always playing catch up. And we're not at the place where we have really crafted the thing, so that being said there's always going to be the disconnection between intention and what we are doing right now and so my invitation to all of us is to time travel.

Marai Larasi[1]

There is nothing new under the sun but there are different ways people can experience the warmth. At Healing Justice London (HJL) we're trying to offer warmth in ways that don't rely on existing ways of being and knowing. We're not campaigning, we're putting forward ideas, philosophies and ways of being which are less familiar to the sites that are doing the necessary campaigning work. We are not organising around what needs to be destroyed but we are organising around what is possible within and outside of us. We do the work of healing, which is inextricably linked to justice, to both resist and build towards futures where we are both free and whole. We recognise that the spaces we might seek in order to access health, healing and recovery in the context of the UK are spaces that continue violence on marginalised communities through colonial practices of harm, exclusion and experimentation. Predetermining who gets to be well, who accesses the things that support our health, which bodies matter, whose pain and suffering is believed, who is worthy and deserving of care and support are among the other oppressive logics.

We merge theory with practice to reimagine wholeness and well-being at the intersection of adversity, disadvantage and oppression. We are led by people of colour, working on the intersections of anti-oppression, health, healing and liberation practice. We seek to undo harms and repair, envision and sustain futures that are free from intimate, interpersonal and structural violence. We are a propositional organisation. While we believe in dismantling current structures, the majority of our work is building towards things that are unknown, unseen and don't have a blueprint. Through trial and error we are figuring out how we generate new sets of conditions and we see that as part of doing something visionary.

We situate ourselves in the practice of healing justice as 'an evolving political framework that ... seeks to transform, intervene and respond to generational trauma and violence in our movements, communities and lives – and to regenerate our traditions of liberatory and resiliency practices that have been lost or stolen'.[2] This framework evolved from organisers including the Black Queer Feminist cultural memory worker Cara Page and the broader Kindred Southern Healing Justice Collective; it gave language to our practice and the long legacy of work within movements and communities in the UK, building capacity for and with the marginalised people with whom we move as part of a continuum. We move with peers in an ecosystem doing this work, including Civic Square, Dark Matter Labs, Skin Deep, Resolve Collective, Migrants in Culture, MAIA Group, 4Front, Kids of Colour, Level Up and No More Exclusions among many others.

We, as people who navigate, live, survive and work to transform conditions of oppression and state violence, know that our very life force and capacity is diminished by oppression. Exposure to ongoing harm and violence, such as racism, ableism and poverty, inflict physical and emotional trauma and sickness that reduce our life expectancy and access to life and living well. These experiences of oppression are often invisiblised, slow and subtle efforts of rupture, unbelonging, breaking down and 'organised abandonment'[3] that steal life. As Ruth Wilson Gilmore, one of the anchors in framing HJL's current strategy, Rehearsing Freedoms, articulates, 'oppression leads to premature death'.[4] The cumulative 'death by a thousand paper cuts' routinely renders us and our movements less equipped, underresourced and unsustainable – leaving us barely able to survive and flourish. Throughout this chapter we invoke and call forward the 'our' and 'we' in acknowledgement of all of us contributing to overturning systems of oppression. This invites us to collapse the neoliberal 'I' and move with a sense of shared and connected struggle in the 'we'.

In our work at HJL, we frame the work of health and healing in its most expansive sense – understanding our inherent need to access connections to our wholeness and to each other. These connections are severed by oppression, including and not limited to loss of our wholeness, bodies, community, life, connection, ways of living, dignity and environment. All of these ruptures mean that the long-termism and sustained efforts of our organising – the organising of structurally oppressed peoples – are habitually broken down, occurring on an individual and collective level.

These confrontations with loss demand that our strategies are subversive in their ways to outwit and outlast our oppressors. This sense of longevity or future thinking and visioning can sometimes feel far removed, even luxurious, when many of us are trying to survive our day-to-day lives. It is precisely because we are designed out of the future that we must see and send ourselves there.

The Politics of Time: Temporality as Strategic Site of Intervention

In 2018, HJL was visioning a lived experience-led research project called A Litany for Survival. We sought to understand and transform the deep, intersecting forms of loss disproportionately (and by design) experienced by racialised and other structurally marginalised communities. The project paid tribute to Audre Lorde's poem by the same name, written during her cancer journey. In the poem, marginalised groups emerge and simultaneously empower and restore themselves with a new understanding of personal and collective power in the midst of loss. When the Covid-19 pandemic hit and we experienced mass loss, some deemed our work as almost 'prophetic' in its timeliness.

What we foresaw was an inevitability. We do grief work because we as marginalised people have already experienced so much loss, and because so many of the fundamental ways the world is arranged would have to come to an end in order to materially realise alternative ways of being. Our task is to find ways to hospice the world as it is and doula in futures rich with deep dignity and justice. We at the margins are already strategising and finding ways to keep each other alive and safe – we are attending to the strategies of survival. Given how pervasive oppression is, what is done to one affects the whole.

Given the disruptive forces of oppression we can understand how our movements are vulnerable to breaking down, because we are chronically broken down. The effectiveness of our movements relies on our sustainability. The onslaught of cumulative violence means our time is stolen away from living and life-giving things, such as joy, connection and creativity, and put towards resistance and survival. This perpetuates our dispossession from self-determination. The engineered precarity of our present means we are less able to enact and realise our futures.

Our work around temporal justice addresses the systemic structures that engineer the theft of time, energy, health and resources. It invites us to consider how our justice work not only enables us to resist but also to be situated in liberation – it enables us to *be*. We see temporal justice in action through how we expand time for those who are most time depleted. When organisations, friends, families and peers resource their communities with things such as the time to adequately grieve, parent or rest, it aligns us with liberation, antiracist and anti-capitalist politics.

Antiracist and anti-capitalist politics are fundamentally about ontology (about our beingness) because all systems of oppression negotiate and undermine our inherent beingness and worthiness. They only affirm our worth by externalising us through productivity, able-bodied health, utility, usefulness or desirability. Therefore, building the capacity to *be* and *be here* is intrinsically linked to liberation work.

We know that some of these concepts might seem abstract but we also want to remember how many Indigenous, Black and people of colour spiritualities and traditions have already been rehearsing and practising these forms of temporal justice/time travelling. For example, ancestral veneration, libation, grief work, prayers, salah, plant medicine journeying, communal rites and rituals as ways to collectively hold and expand time. In Islam, and many mindfulness practices, when you go into prayer or meditative spaces you go into a space of timelessness. Part of our work is repairing these spiritual, anti-colonial, non-Eurocentric practices of resource and nourishment, collapsing the 'I think therefore I am' to 'we are, so it is'.

Strategies for Temporal Justice

As we understand the ways that time is used against us, we have to find ways to liberate this distorted use of time towards a political strategy.

Staci Haines, the author of *The Politics of Trauma* and one of our movement building partners at HJL, reminds us that to become visionary we have to know that better is out there, and to be loving we have to be able to be present with what is here. For those of us who live on the fringes, we want to offer each other pathways to other possibilities while loving each other right now. Oppression diminishes the love between us and convinces us we are unlovable. This ruptures our coming together.

Below we outline three key strategies from our learnings and decades of community organising on how we might create communal and structural capacity for time and temporal justice:

1. Strategic pacing – a dynamic and appropriate use of timeliness.

2. Strategy as solidarity economy – creating time among ourselves.
3. Being in time – offering ourselves and each other our presence and aliveness.

Strategic Pacing

For those of us organising in social justice, for years we've been hearing about the need to slow down as a way of refusing the capitalist and Eurocentric idea of urgency culture. At HJL, we recognise the importance of pacing our work and supporting ourselves to unlearn the deep, internalised belief that time is linear and informed by capitalist logic, and therefore loss of time as a failure. While the heart of our work is about sustainability, we couple slowing down with understanding the need for rhythm and congruence with our context. We organise our work across seasons and cycles as an act of growing time and spaciousness. This includes understanding grief work as a fundamental practice to help us sense and know completion instead of infinite accumulation and perpetuity. Phasing and iterating offers us the generosity of experimentation and learning for rigorous work that has no blueprint. It enables us to create a buffer around some of the work that we know is critical and urgent. There may be moments where we have to work at pace, urgently and critically, because our social and political contexts demand it. As a health and healing justice organisation, moments such as the start of the pandemic or lockdown are critical and opportune times to galvanise. Likewise, mass-disabling times throughout Covid-19, mass austerity and oppression mean that we cannot be naive or irresponsible in presuming that all of our work would fit into a 9–5 capitalist work structure. Holding the tension of when we have to be responsive and reactive while also creating long-term visions and strategies to phase our work allows us to say *this is possible right now* and work within as much of our capacity as possible.

We time travel towards resourcing ourselves and each other by finding portals and spaces where we can stop or grow time. At HJL, our practice spaces are a key example of this in application. This space is an intentional pause (e.g. our weekly breath circle space or restorative yoga). We often open by inviting everyone who attends to consider it as a protected time, a time for pouring in and a time for engaging in mindfulness or spiritual practices that resources us.

These acts of community care are not social justice theories. They are ways of being that we have to reconnect and remember with to recontextualise for our times, unlearning the deep individualisation and fractures to foster a relational attunement to one another.

Strategy as Solidarity Economy

In the context of a finite world with finite resources, without rein-forcing sentiments of scarcity, we need pathways and maps towards generative and abundant futures. We know that the ways in which we live, exist and currently operate are unsustainable. Racial capi-talism is on its last legs and everything that it has infected is feeling that deterioration. The level of change and social overhaul we need in these times of cumulative and escalating crisis demands that we have bold strategies to respond. It means that we have to mass mobi-lise and organise effectively in order to be able to have fierce and spacious coalitions. This is both an act of time travel backwards and forwards, to connect our struggles and strategies, as well as a lateral move to join up our current resistance and visions.

In our work, Movement Medicine, we have a two-pronged approach. In the first, we bring together movement leaders across sectors and struggles, intergenerationally and at different stages of their organising, to undergo an embodied leadership process. Here we practise being leaders together, practice embodied allyship, expe-rience mutuality and make commitments and declarations towards collective visions. We practise, through somatics, how we might move together even through conflict and contradictions while ensuring that our actions are aligned with our values. Following this space, we have Movement Medicine Labs to open-source learn-ing, hack at tensions and be peers for one another. These Movement Medicine spaces also train us to become community first responders through abolition and somatic work so we can skilfully hold our communities and grow political education and practise together in such distressing times.

When our organising holds movements as a place where everyone has a role to play, and we are surrounded by enough players from the grassroots to allies in sites of power, we have to identify a strategy. It anchors how we realistically work towards aligned visions and goals.

This approach resists the colonial *divide and conquer* which pushes us towards competition; instead it helps us reach towards collaboration. We must make sure that we are surrounded by opportunities for bidirectional learning, where we hack and explore recurring tensions and breakdowns in our movements and organising and are able to learn with and from one another. This enables us to move progressively, as opposed to starting from scratch, and mitigates the time theft of re-experiencing the common injuries and wounds of movement work that set us back and break us down.

We recognise that clunkiness and conflict will be part of this work so we need to become skilled in how we have both the pre-forgiveness and the capaciousness to learn, iterate, make mistakes, grow and have a healthier relationship with what we do. When we identify strategy, it enables us to centre ourselves and stay on our purpose and mission with more potential to navigate some of the necessary messiness of this work. It anchors us to where we can go together and invites us to consider how we each become leaders in supporting the health of the entire ecosystem, including ourselves.

Great strategies are not enabled by ideas, visions and frameworks alone; they are made possible by skilful individuals with leadership qualities who continuously realign with purpose. It's often like playing jazz, where the performance relies on every musician honing their craft and discipline so that when they come together, everybody shines and what they create is dazzling. No musician is greater than the other and each one enables the other towards new and greater possibilities.

On a movement and mass-organising level, strategies create time and free us up to focus and position ourselves where we are best placed to act. They encourage us to extend and build trust regarding our shared purpose in the ecosystem of change and justice. This is reliant on developing approaches to movement making that are holistic and expansive and hold movements as multilayered with multiple entry points. Against this critical backdrop, we don't get to set the timeline for change; however, we can create our own rhythms. We have to be pragmatic and develop a relay approach to how we slow down, resource ourselves, pick up pace, act and show up in solidarity to allow others to do the same.

We also recognise that as people who have been harmed and made to live precariously, building strategies and operating strategically isn't always available to us.

Being in Time

Oppression creates conditions of chronic stress which people cannot survive (on a mental, physical and spiritual level). To survive oppression and tolerate the ongoing violence, we, in different ways, come out of time – because it is not safe to be here. Physiologically our body finds ways to keep us alive by vacating time, and if prolonged this contributes to the detriment of our aliveness. Trauma and stress responses, by keeping us out of time, can often leave us in two places: anxious about the future or grief-ridden about the past. Oppression keeps us from being *here* and the quality of our connections, both with ourselves and each other, become less of a resource or source of restoration. The fundamental human need for belonging and connection through community is made less possible, compromising the sustained connection needed for movement work and transformative cultures.

We honour our stress and survival responses because they have kept us alive. Yet we invite an understanding of whether these responses are congruent with our current reality. Being discerning about whether our stress responses are appropriate right now supports us to be loving towards ourselves when our survival and stress responses kick in and to access the types of resourcing and support we might need. In contrast, it can also help us identify when the stress or survival response is not needed and when we might be able to choose a different response. This process connects us with our agency and our capacity to be consensual – it is life affirming because this helps us access more life.

When we are traumatised, certain capacities become diminished. Two things in particular hinder our movement and liberation work. First, in a heightened state of stress or distress we go into survival mode. This is an appropriate response which happens on a physiological level. We are less able to hear one another and our bodies respond in ways designed to protect us. This makes it harder for us to be collaborative and situated in a *we*. Likewise, we end up using more of our short-term memory (the immediate) and rely less on our long-term memory as we need to address what's happening right now to preserve energy. This means that contexts can collapse and the arc of our relationships can feel less familiar – this is incompatible with sustainable movement building. It can be hard for us to trust and see a future beyond the moment. Often in these states, when we are considering the future, our perspective comes from an underresourced and depleted space as opposed to a creative, visionary space which lends itself to the abundant futures we want to build. This does not mean that we are not creative even in our survival. Often the most marginalised are surviving in genius and skilful ways. What this offers is an invitation to explore what else becomes possible when we're more resourced.

We ground our work within the frame of liberatory trauma work because we understand how the wellness industrial complex aligns with forms of capitalism that continue to exploit us, especially when we are sick or vulnerable. Therefore, we hold that doing trauma work is not about becoming adaptive to oppression. We align ourselves with the groundbreaking and leading approach that our partners Lumos Transforms call 'alchemical resilience'. Alchemical resilience being 'the flexible strength to heal, overcome adversity, and change systems of inequity and oppression into places where we thrive'.[5] This is why we recognise that the work of creating temporal justice through strategic efforts is made possible when we also engage with trauma work and our own abilities to grow. Holding the aforementioned ways of working and engaging with temporal justice, we wanted to introduce a concrete campaign and body of work that brings together these issues of temporal justice. Within our Deaths by Welfare campaign, built with disabled activists, we use the charting of time to document and evidence structural violence, while looking at a specific case study into how bureaucratic and slow violence steals time. Deaths by Welfare is in its first cycle, embedded in our larger vision of prototyping radical alternatives and community health.

Case Study: Deaths by Welfare Timeline

Time is key to how violence works. Bursts of spectacular violence are often the outcome of longer, slower, enduring forms of violence – the kind where harms accumulate gradually over time.[6] Violence that inflicts harm in slow motion is important because it makes causes harder to see and name – something which is used as a weapon by those with power (states, corporations, the elite) to deny accountability. An important way in which this shows up for us is in our Deaths by Welfare project, which investigates people's deaths resulting from welfare state violence in the UK, and particularly from the welfare reforms associated with state austerity (punitive policies introduced after 2008, made up of conditionality, sanctions and assessments outsourced to corporations). This is a context that has crafted and reproduced intense conditions of hostility towards disabled people (especially those who claim welfare) to justify erosion of public funding, punitive policies and state abandonment, making life, for many, unliveable.

Welfare reform that enacts slower forms of violence that obscure simple formulations of cause and effect, allowing accountability to be avoided, is well known to many disabled people. Disabled people know that to analyse welfare state violence we need to be attuned to the ways that harms accumulate slowly, over time. Thus, any analysis of welfare state violence and deaths, but also of accountability and justice, must focus on the analysis developed by disabled people regarding the welfare system. A core part of this work has been the co-creation of a timeline tracing the slow accumulation of welfare state violence (co-designed with John Pring, editor of the Disability News Service and a disabled person, and with the expertise of disabled activists, campaigners and artists – Dolly Sen, Ellen Clifford and Rick Burgess).

Our timeline is made up of largely publicly available documents (though ones that are often hard to find) that relate to the deaths of disabled people claiming or trying to claim benefits. The current timeline goes back to the 1970s to trace the conditions that laid some of the foundations for what came to be known as 'welfare reform', but the welfare system as one arm of wider state violence, and one with a colonial history, is much longer than this.

Reading the timeline in chronological order reveals a slow, bureaucratic accumulation of harm. The timeline makes it possible to follow the introduction of a specific policy or practice through to its delayed effects, and it is thus a tool to make visible slow violence. Yet while the timeline is linear, it can be navigated in non-linear ways, to represent experiences and analyses of temporality informed by disability and illness – the 'time travel' of 'crip time' – a non-linear 'backward and forward acceleration' of long intervals and 'abrupt endings'.[7] By doing this, we show that some things were predicted before they happened (e.g. the early warnings of deaths that when read in retrospect feel eerie), while others, including many people's deaths, were only known about publicly long after people had died.

Many early warnings of harm came from disabled people, another example of foresight coming from deep insight and knowledge generated through lived experience. This is the time travel and prophecies of disabled peoples' knowledge that Leah Lakshmi Piepzna-Samarasinha writes about in *The Future Is Disabled* – where crip futurism is visioning a future of disabled love, joy and liberation while surviving in an ableist world where disabled people die because we're told they don't matter. Disabled people's knowledge is essential for our collective liberation. One example of this relates to time. Leah Lakshmi Piepzna-Samarasinha shows how the skills that chronically ill folks craft to navigate the durational ongoing time of chronicity have so much to teach us in our current context of chronic enduring grief.

Co-creating the timeline has provided a method to piece together seemingly unconnected singular events, along with key evidence that only came to light years after it occurred, allowing us to track patterns across time which would remain hidden if we focused only on individuals' deaths. This has helped us to see that time is key to understanding everyday, bureaucratic and institutional welfare state violence, a violence which kills people. Time plays a part in the production of harm – cumulative, attritional suffering that dispro-portionately impacts certain groups of people, including disabled people – as well as being used as a strategy by the government who weaponise time to avoid accountability and deny justice.

Our timeline and work is guided by this map – retelling the history of the welfare state and welfare reform to document how decisions made by those with power became the origins of pain and the causes of death, and to trace the collective resistance (through protest, knowledge production, care networks and mutual aid) of disabled people.

Travelling towards Antiracist Futures

Our opening invitation is one to time travel because we oscillate between the worlds we long for and the conditions and contexts we have. We share our reflections and strategies not to hold us hostage to an unknown future but rather to see what of that future we can access now as a way to offer each other and ourselves life. Our com-mitment at HJL to create capacity for transformation emerged out of reckoning with temporal justice – because of the resounding ways we find ourselves outside of and without time. We cannot begin to do the work of healing justice without having the capacity to self-de-termine what we are calling in. Temporal justice and time travelling, as strategies for robust movement making, are already things we practise as part of our own survival. Now with intentionality, how might our time travelling together pull the future forwards? Our insights already help us envision alternatives, but those in power tell us what the future is going to be. Not only do we see the future first but we want to be there. As we explore *growing time* and *being here*, let us be curious about how temporal justice can make our liberation work as both a map of the future we are constructing and the arrow on which we travel together.

> We'll let you guys prophesy
> We'll let you guys prophesy
> We gon' see the future first.
>
> Frank Ocean, Nikes

7

Creative and Embodied Approaches to Antiracism

Voices that Shake

We invite you to:

Unclench your jaw.
Drop your shoulders.
Take three deep breaths.
Roll your shoulders back three times.

Choose at least one other place to do this while reading this chapter.

Decide when you feel the need to pause in response to what you've read.

Background

Cultural practices within racialised communities are often deemed and demonised by the state as inferior or subversive. Mainstream culture is part of how race, racism and capitalism are reproduced. Under the present hostile environment of 'culture wars', asserting and affirming the value of insurgent culture and practising counter-culture becomes ever more important. Shake! recognises the need to have a critical engagement with culture and the need to maintain radical/traditional practices of culture/creativity. In our Rep the Road programme a core question we ask of ourselves is: what are the cultural practices that have enabled us to be here today, to survive? What ancestral and familial wisdoms are useful for us to remember and resurrect?

Shake!'s approach to antiracism lies within an analysis of global structures which leaves space to explore and think about where we are from, how we are impacted and how interconnected we are. In weaving together legacies and traditions of resistance, our lived experiences and participatory pedagogies, Shake! encourages and emboldens participants to build liberatory maps for themselves.

Over the 14 years since Shake! was founded, our free-to-attend courses, skill-shares and trainings have centred a holistic, proactive and visionary reimagining in response to the urgency of the socio-political landscape we find ourselves in. Course themes have ranged from topics such as state violence, gentrification, mental health, media literacy, climate justice, food justice and reparations, with a racial analysis emphasised throughout. Shakers! have then gone on to lead in programming cultural productions, multi-artform showcases and training events, as well as forming and connecting to new and existing artist and activist collectives. Led and sustained by a group of intergenerational facilitators from Black and global majority communities, and from different creative and organising backgrounds, Shake! also offers ongoing pastoral support and mentorship.

Our vision for how we believe change happens is:

- Using a model of personal transformation and structural change to challenge established imbalanced power bases and reimagining new infrastructures in opposition to capitalism and colonialism.
- Building holistic decolonial educational programmes and creative campaigns to foster a catalytic and self-determined community of creative organisers/leaders embedded in, and led by, the grassroots.
- Working together to cultivate transformative justice, systemic change and community accountability.
- Working collectively to centre the leadership and solutions of the marginalised, to uplift and politicise the role that young people of global majority have and to prefigure the world we

would like to live in: diverse, just, sustainable, community-led and resilient.

Antiracist Creativity

Creativity is in everything we do: our pedagogical approach, our art, our activism. We recognise that creativity is moving and it moves us; we know that in order to enact change we need to do things differently. The education system has failed us, the arts sector has failed us, mainstream activism has failed us. Therefore, we embrace creativity and our imagining of different futures and possibilities.

There are many artistic and cultural practices we draw upon within Shake! spaces. These include: poetry, prose writing, spoken word, film, music and DJing, dance, collage, zinemaking, play, outdoor activities, martial arts, yoga, breathwork and meditation. Our foundational art forms are: spoken word and the power of coming to voice; film and moving images that harnesses young people's analyses to form visual art with technical ingenuity; image-making through collaging and zines; vocal expression through song, breathwork and hollering; and bodywork that supports us to inhabit our bodies as people who are brutalised out of them.

In these Shake! spaces, we centre historical and contemporary examples of radical art/organising from the Black and global majority diaspora. This helps us connect to legacies of antiracism work that have affected us on a sensory level: those that have a track record of generating change; that have galvanised movements; and that stand as inspirations offering clear strategic guidance for the next generations. Anecdotal examples offered from facilitators and participants alike of lived experience open up possibilities to explore our identities, cultural heritage and some of the racialised tensions encountered along the way.

Annick (Shake!'s current Legacy programme manager) references how many of these conversations about racism were centred around the importance of connecting with people my age who had the same experience of being children of immigrants, having parents who had migrated to Europe at some point. I remember Farzana [Khan] talking about police presence in a meeting of Bengali elders in East London and connecting this to intergenerational trauma and history. Shake! really brought that global majority idea of sitting in a room together and the racism that we experience being specific to how we're Black, we're Asian, we're whatever, but ultimately, we have all experienced racism. And that's what we have in common under white supremacy: intergenerational trauma and migration experience, all of these elements come together.

The approach to these conversations is pivotal in understanding the expanse of racism: making space for a shared insight between academic framings and personal experiences. Distilling the lived experience of racism outside of its theoretical context allows for a type of critical analysis that engages a multiplicity of peoples at a foundational level.

Annick continues:

I was really not used to talking about racism in terms of the body, healing. I was really good at researching it, analysing it, rationalising it, but not really at asking myself what is the impact on my body. 'Where does this live in me?' 'How has that potentially impacted my health?' ... Having thoughts such as 'all oppression is interconnected' in the room gave me so much confidence and so many tools to talk about racism as a beast with multiple heads: the oil industry, neocolonialism, capitalism ... All these different ways that racism manifests itself and participates in other forms of oppression. How racism can look different, in different ways, was really eye opening and helped me round up a structural analysis that I was struggling to put together.

As Annick states, Shake! rejects the 'ways that whiteness ultimately is comfortable with Black and global majority people talking about

racism: either the crying traumatised victim – trauma porn performance for white eyes; or the cold, analytical, academic way where
you have to bring facts and numbers as long as your analytical frame
is agreed by white men'.

When considering how antiracism shows up in their own life,
tiff (Shake!'s former co-producer and design lead), who first joined
Shake! for our *Healing the Cuts* course, states:

> We're all conditioned to be racist, so it's this constant reprogram-
> ming and practising of what does it mean to be antiracist? I had
> a deep self-hatred. I was taught to hate myself, to other myself, to
> make myself small, to assimilate, for so long. It's a continuous life
> practice for me to not be anti-Black and to be pro-Black and to be
> antiracist.

This sense of being atomised and minoritised within white supremacist environments is a familiar experience. Even for those who
grow up within strong Black and global majority communities, the
sentiment of white supremacy, through the material and abstract
infrastructures of racial capitalism, permeates every fabric of social
reality.

In terms of how antiracism practice shows up within Shake!, tiff
continues:

> Antiracism informs anything and everything … we discuss, inter-
> rogate and learn through all of the things that we do … how racism
> in all its forms impacts, manifests. How we call racism out, or how
> it is taking place presently, what it feels like in our bodies … 'Let's
> name it', 'How does that feel?', 'How do we take care of ourselves
> to navigate it?' … Because once we leave this Shake! space, as soon
> as we come out that door, it's going to hit us.

Paula Serafini, a mentor for our recent youth-led research report,
comments that:

Shake! participants disrupt mainstream narratives, but also challenge preconceptions on both art and activism, which in the UK can often be associated to white and middle-class identities, viewpoints, spaces, and aesthetics. Shake! brought forward a different idea of art activism that decentres the most visible forms of action and instead proposes a more holistic approach, valuing different forms of activism, expression and intervention with the aim of generating change on individual, community and structural levels.

From these intimate, intensive and nurturing workshop and conversation spaces, Shake! has been able to further intervene in antiracist and liberatory praxis by offering showcases of this work to a wider public. Annick speaks to why she believes performances at Shake! showcases are powerful:

> Because they're affirming – another way to talk about racism and antiracism. We're not asking anything of whiteness. The way we express ourselves feels like dignity in its purest form where you're just not afraid to talk about trauma if you want to. You're not afraid to talk about your experience. You're not justifying yourself. You're not asking for anything because whiteness has nothing for us. We're not giving them the role of saviour, we're not giving them the role of main character … we are the main characters of our story.

Applying the Pillars of Shake!

Our work around antiracism is drawn together under 'Pillars of Shake!':

- Nurturing Trust – Radical Cultures of Kindness.
- Radical Pedagogy – Centring Arts, Culture and Play.
- Moving from Participation to Presence – Encountering Our Wholeness.

- Movement Work – Embodying Liberatory Practice.
- Nourishment – Nurturing through Nature and Food.
- Sustaining Ourselves – Restorative Space and Living Library.
- Community Care work – Wellness and Care Pool.

Annick describes how pillars such as 'Sustaining Ourselves', 'Radical Pedagogy' and 'Nourishment' work in practice as

a combination of all the methodologies, the tools, the actual objects and the way the space is set up, both in a physical sense and intangible way ... Sitting down doing a guided meditation I remember Farzana mentioned talking to your inner child. I got super emotional, super choked up because it was honestly the first space in my life where I thought about my inner child, talked to my child self, and really seriously committed to doing that. And the thing that came up was pain and injustice. And I needed to take a minute, but then you get up and you walk to the table and there's a book: an image of a Black woman, *This Bridge Called My Back*. And this title hits you, and then you can step out into a little garden space and you touch plants to recuperate. And then you realise, oh, that's what my child self used to do. Everything makes sense.

This work of antiracism and discovering our place within it – our complicity within systemic racism, our sites of privilege, our struggle to combat racism – is not an easy or comfortable reckoning. Annick describes how the care-filled work that goes into designing these spaces can help 'nurture trust', help build 'radical cultures of kindness', help us 'move from participation to presence and encounter our wholeness' and help us be 'sustained through restorative spaces and care pools':

Everything in the pillars of Shake!, the experience of what is in the room, draws out this really difficult work. But at the same time in the best way possible so you can talk about it safely in a way that makes sense enough. And most importantly, you're not alone. People can finish your sentences. People understand. I remember being told multiple times: 'Try not to apologise.' 'Be vulnerable, because it's an honour for us for you to be vulnerable around us.' This all eases the sensory, physical and mental journey that is connecting within us – for me, for the first time – with questions of where does antiracism and racism live in me and show up in my life.

Under the pillar of 'Radical Pedagogy – Centring Arts, Culture and Play' is the recognition that we are deserving of and worthy of joy; a recognition that many antiracist spaces neglect this core principle of connecting (to each other, to nature, to our bodies) to the detriment of fostering a trusting and enlivened community. Embracing moments of radical joy can be key in enabling us to process intense moments, to (re)connect to our bodies and our purpose, and to offer relief from the pressures and traumas that antiracist work brings. Centring radical joy is an intentional act which, for some, can just be the simple noticing of everyday small pleasures, recognising that feelings of joy are not fixed or a constant.

tiff speaks to the importance and intentionality of games in the Shake! space and how they are used to punctuate the sessions and offer pauses: moments of relief to intensive moments as well as invitations for us to (re)connect to our child-like playful selves through laughter, joy, dance, music, art and expression:

You didn't feel like a fool ... Even though the last time you really played games like this in a community, you were like five. There's no way I want to be playing these games in groups in my early twenties. I was just like, 'What is this?' But fun and play are contagious, so you just end up surfacing that playful side to you. That inner child that wants to still play and connect in this way comes out. It was so vital to actually help us process what we had just gone through in a heavy session. It's almost like we needed to play to shake it out of our body and also bring back in that laughter, to connect us again and to communally soothe, not just self-soothe.

Games and short play exercises provide opportunities to practise and become skilled in community movement making and resistance work. They provide safe spaces for us to rehearse and enhance our activism, deepen our organising and make our resistance robust. Making space for joy, play, song, dance, art, movement and ritual, with and through our bodies, regardless of ability, supports us to nurture community and strengthen our sustainability.

Joy and play help us remember who we are even though we are forced to transform/transmute under oppression for survival. It allows many of us who survived, and who are surviving oppressions, to reclaim our lives and to move towards liberated futures. It is therefore crucial for us to pace our programmes with games and prioritise joy as part of learning and relaxing. Our political spaces are more powerful when we can let go of our fears and connect with our inner child. Our joy is political. Releasing it is a radical act which sustains our movements.

Honour your grief
Honour your rage
Honour your fear
Honour the knowledge systems and memories that live in you
Pay homage to your lineages
Honour your awakening and desire for something else.

Teju Adeleye

Each one of the pillars of Shake!'s practice is enhanced by, and draws upon, the principle that we are far more effective organisers when we are able to invite our bodies into the room. By recognising and taking note of ourselves as full human beings (mind, spirit and body) we move from the individualistic, dismembered, dominator way of being (Descartes: 'I think therefore I am') to a more embodied community remembering (Ubuntu: 'I am because we are'). From this space we are more able and open to receive Indigenous wisdom that teaches against a hierarchy of human knowledge and which allows for ancient, futurist, ancestral learning from plants, animals and the cosmos.

tiff speaks to how conversations detailing the traumas of racism can reveal deep emotions and how it is important to honour and hold these emotions:

> We've been conditioned to try and stop someone showing so much pain, like crying, and we are meant to soothe straight away to make it stop. Instead, it's almost like this space allowed us to just let people fall apart if they needed to, and to be felt like they were going to be held at the end of releasing all that pain. We needed to let that come out because of how much pain we're carrying.

The interposing of movement games, food and moments of joy, to bring our body back into the conversation/space, compliments this experience of collective vulnerability.

Having studied antiracist pedagogy in academia, Annick also notes how it can be

> really easy to fall into talking about racism the way racism wants to be talked about. Even in a room of global majority people, there's an acceptable way that white supremacy will have you talk about racism: bringing it down to intentions, to interpersonal relations, to ignorance, detaching yourself; asking you to talk about it in a rational, analytical way because emotional stuff doesn't have value. If I tried to mention anything about my own experience, academics around me were really uncomfortable … As Grada Kilomba notes in 'Who Can Speak': there are ways that are valid and which carry information and all the ways that are considered not valid and not valuable.

Reuben Liebeskind, who first experienced Shake! when attending our Healing the Cuts course, reflects on their experience of being invited to feel their full selves:

For many of us who live with trauma, the connection between the mind and the body is numbed. To reawaken that connection is so challenging because it means feeling pain that's been carried unacknowledged and alone so long ... When we open up these emotional spaces we have more room in our lives for love, joy, reclamation, and truth. We are empowered to imagine a world free of violence and fear. What Shake! taught me is that most of the time, pain just wants to be felt, to be seen by others.

These reflections echo a common creative prompt used in Shake! spaces, Audre Lorde's call in 'A Litany for Survival':

when we are silent
we are still afraid
So it is better to speak
remembering
we were never meant to survive.

International and Intergenerational Learnings

From our very first course, Shake! has intentionally used both a national and an international lens to explore historical legacies of colonialism and present-day manifestations. Our pilot course engaged young participants in discussion around systematic racism using the stories of Stephen Lawrence, in the UK, and Ken Saro-Wiwa, in Nigeria, and allowed us to ask questions and draw parallels regarding how the British state is complicit in each of these very different examples of racist violence.

Key moments of learning for Shake! have included engaging with the International Social Movement for Afrikan Reparations from 2010 till the present; connecting with and offering solidarity to front-line communities at COP21 in Paris 2015; attending INCITE Color of Violence 4, Chicago 2015; attending and presenting at the Allied Media Conference, Detroit 2016; and connecting with global majority communities as part of Platform's Dance the Guns to

Silence series of events (2015, 2020). Our work with the Stuart Hall Foundation for the Black Activism Map in 2018 enabled us to showcase some of this learning to a large audience. The 'Rep the Road' series of community dialogues and workshops initiated as a part of this process were then translated in engagements with activists and artists overseas where this pedagogy was deepened in skill-shares with communities in the Gambia (2018) and Kenya (2020).

Within the current Shake! team, our pedagogy has naturally evolved to embrace remote working. This has enabled the team to connect from different parts of the world (France, Spain, Senegal, Mexico) and different contexts that we might be in. Team members are also part of collectives and groups outside of Shake! and outside of a UK context which helps to bring an international lens and insight, particularly around moments of racial violence and uprisings, and a globally informed but locally responsive approach to our work. Within the space of our courses, deliberate time is made to acknowledge, connect to and be guided by who is in the room and by our various cultural, diasporic and Indigenous wisdoms. An international antiracist praxis means thinking deeply about global structures and the connection of the core and the periphery; about how migrant communities through forced assimilation experience disconnect to 'back home' and how we all need to be internationalists.

We must also acknowledge that compartmentalisation across generations reproduces oppression. When we hold the young as *only* 'the future' we deny young people the opportunity to build and move with us in the present, with us now. In order to build holistic and wholesome futures that hold all of us, we must engage in the wisdom and experience of our elders and the insight and zeal of our youth simultaneously.

Oppression is successful in rupturing connection: as we see in the dismemberment of our people's bodies, communities, environments, narratives and more. Intergenerational building provides both a pathway and a portal to (borrowing from the titles of some of our courses): *survive the system*; *remember, reimagine, reparations*; reclaim *head space*; *repair the road*; and *heal the cuts*. Intergenerationality serves as a central methodology to move together to places where the logic and apparatus of disconnection are diminished.

We share across and within generations as a way to collapse imbalanced hierarchies, to challenge power dynamics (and respectability politics) and to honour knowledge and ancestral wisdom by connecting with ways of being that existed before us, while making sure they continue to do so fluidly beyond us. We create opportunities for this to be built upon and recontextualised based on need and appropriateness. We reach backwards to send forwards.

The concept of researching our own families and archiving our own history becomes a holistic act of cultural reparative justice, done for ourselves without the power dynamic of a white anthropological gaze. Long-time Shake! collaborator and guest facilitator Kinsi Abdulleh shared the Numbi Arts' project Coming Here, Being Here on our recent ENRGY! course. Kinsi explained that the essence and intention of Numbi's project is about family sharing stories and how, because of (neo)colonial efforts to make our language and cultures extinct, language can be a ground of violent rupture for our intergenerational relationships. The radical potentiality of our ancestral narratives as knowledge systems is thus diluted and requires a constant and deliberate vigilance to resist, to notice, to value and to hold these narratives in the present so that they may guide us towards liberatory futures.

Radical connection requires time: an ongoing curiosity and commitment that isn't always easy, especially when our very human fears, anxieties and distress show up. Building community spaces can inadvertently reproduce dynamics of power, by presenting some of us as 'experts', 'celebrity activist influencers' and 'educators'. It is sometimes necessary to have people guide and scaffold spaces where we are building together – especially with communities that are informed by trauma – but it is important that we also seek to practise ways to disrupt hierarchies of knowledge production. This means finding supportive ways to uplift and embolden each other's agency and intuition, wisdom and the expertise of our youth.

Radical connection is a non-extractive and non-transactional entry point that acknowledges and honours the reality of how interconnected and interdependent we are and that we have the ability to envision and build together. Non-hierarchical and horizontal teaching and sharing takes into account the way power and privilege has to be redistributed and levelled in an equitable way which can be sustained – particularly so as not to overwhelm the young, absolve elders of their own responsibilities and to resist any replication of marginalisation within our own communities. In Shake! we consistently look to the possibility of a dynamic relationship between leaders and participants, as we see group members become facilitators and facilitators become group members.

We can resist the division and individualisation that systemic power urges by identifying it through political education; questioning how it shows up between us; actively practising how to stop it replicating by building personal transformation in community; and then strategically taking this praxis into different spaces and contexts where systemic power is present. When this tactic is scaled up it can, and will, cause structures to disrupt and dismantle.

We have borne witness to the ripple effect of a whole generation of community organisers situated in different institutions and influential places of power carrying this pedagogy. This is how we believe systemic change happens and how we can foster long-term impact – deep, long-term work with smaller groups where it is ultimately people who are changing first from the inside and then carrying this pedagogy within them. This focus on quality of engagement rather than quantity is a radical position to take in the world of youth work where most organisations are encouraged by funders and authorities to reach big numbers. With no real mechanisms to define what 'reach' means, this approach inevitably leads to a small and diluted impact. In contrast to this, the small-scale, difficult relationships with individuals often take place unseen and it is only years later that we witness the full fruits of this impact.

Sustaining Our Energies and Movements

As part of sustainable co-facilitation practice, we recognise the importance of working with and being fluid around people's needs.

We believe this will only be possible if there are habits and cultures of self- and collective accountability. We seek to build cultures that don't reproduce harm and work to minimise the impact of harm, especially around divisions of labour and burnout – both of which are often sources of collective breakdown. The restoration of disturbed boundaries helps in supporting autonomy, as opposed to simply existing in reaction to the conditions of racism. Recognising when boundaries have been crossed as a racialised person in a racist world can help preserve energy in our communities, organising to address the exhaustion (particularly of Black women) in care work and to expand our capacity.

Shake!'s journey has necessitated addressing internal movement dynamics and sustainability, community care, intention, heartbreak and isolation and loneliness, navigating legacy work at a distance and navigating grief, as well as asking questions about how to best showcase and disseminate our work in a meaningful and responsible manner. Self-care for ourselves as facilitators, as people holding space for other people's experiences and trauma, is important to nurture long-term sustainability and safety.

We recognised the need to pause, recentre and gather our energies most pressingly around 2017. This was a time of bereavement, a moment of rupture for our internal team and also a time spent responding to the Grenfell tragedy. Our 2017 Movement Medicine course provided a programme for our wider community to address these healing and reparative needs, including sessions on: centring community narratives and language; organising under surveillance and Prevent; building mechanisms of accountability; radical archiving and community documenting; fundraising skill-shares; building alternative economies; community skills and resource mapping; moving beyond fear, shame, guilt and anger; and sustaining ourselves/movements and well-being.

As an antiracist community, we continue to navigate and work our way through these issues, developing and implementing policies and accountability procedures to do this work responsibly. Responding to the Covid-19 pandemic and Black Lives Matter uprisings from 2020 onwards has necessitated us to hold space for each other in new ways; to listen and respond in new ways, consistently creating and shifting capacity; supporting each other with care packages, emergency support, resource distribution, check-ins, embodied groundings and regular strategy sessions; and holding each other accountable with grace. Through our interconnectedness at a distance and in isolation, we move inwardly and extend ourselves outwardly towards a better working practice, team accountability and confidence to recognise and then challenge practice in other spheres when it does not align with these principles.

By 'liberatory praxis' we mean praxis as the embodiment of liberation – a practice that we do daily in everything we relate to, what we say, what we do with our bodies, our actions and our thoughts. Many times in movement spaces we do not have the space or capacity for honest self-critique and improvement. We have seen how this lack of process and skill to hold critique has dismantled and broken down collectives. Constantly trying to embody liberatory practice also means critiquing ourselves with the intention of doing better; naming and moving with the importance of accountability. This continual struggling and grappling is what we and all antiracist groups must do to make ending neocolonialism possible. Rehearsing in real time prepares the ground for us to be led by one another. By undoing neoliberal and neocolonial practices in our social relations we transform our lives away from the alienated and commodified existences we're driven into; we revolutionise how we relate to one another; we co-develop and co-realise the tools to build strong, inclusive movements.

To meet the growing crises in our communities this work does need to be scaled up and expanded locally, nationally and internationally. Connections to our diaspora communities need to be solid and rooted, and our international solidarity needs to be rigorous, accountable and taking full care to navigate the pitfalls of saviourism, privilege and dominance. Furthermore, as the UK and USA become increasingly isolated and recognised as international pariahs for their support and fostering of colonial genocides – and as former colonised peoples find voice, rise up and form alliances together – it becomes an ever more urgent and even existential duty for us to culturally connect in true solidarity with our international siblings. The many non-liberatory (neocolonial, neoliberal, careerist, extractivist, white saviourist/supremacist, top-down, corporate-funded, state-aligned, counter-revolutionary) attempts to undermine, whitewash, water down and appropriate this essential and true solidarity must be resisted at every turn. In applying some of the antiracist principles and insurgent cultural practices mentioned in this chapter it is hoped that wider movements can maintain integrity and build genuine connection based on mutual interest, mutual survival and the shared reciprocity of culture and creativity necessary to heal our world.

8
Building an Antiracist Tenants Union

Greater Manchester Tenants Union

Greater Manchester Tenants Union (GMTU) emerged from the backdrop of ongoing resistance to estate clearances and the transformation of working-class districts by gentrification, which are part of the story of housing struggles that can serve to mobilise residents and supporters from the liberal and radical left. The stigmatisation of places leading to neglect by private and social landlords creates a slow violence which has been the challenge we are working to address. Activism in response to the 'housing crisis' often fails to address structural inequalities based on race, migration and gender, and the lived experience of those at the sharp end of state violence created by reliance on the market to meet housing needs is central to building a successful tenants' union.

In this chapter we reflect on the ongoing process of building an antiracist tenants' union in Moss Side, Manchester and what our learning offers the broader movement for housing justice. Our approach is informed by our own experiences organising in mainstream politics, trade unions, Black organisations and other campaigns.[1] We have also drawn from the organising experiences of housing justice campaigns. This has included historical insights[2] as well as working with existing tenants' unions through joint events. We also draw on our own understandings of structural racism in education, employment and criminal justice as well as housing.

Drawing from recent organising experiences and our reading of archival material about resistance to slum clearance in Moss Side in the early 1970s, we hope to provide important lessons for antiracist organising. This includes the importance of building a membership organisation for tenants that is independent of other stakeholders, that adopts a collective action approach and that recognises other issues that members face by providing solidarity with other experiences of racism and political education.

Building the Tenants' Union

Moss Side tenants' union was the first branch of the GMTU, set up in 2017 with a broad set of demands around housing justice. Initially the most active members owned their own homes, which differed significantly to the local area where 43 per cent live in social housing, 35 per cent in private rented and the rest in houses owned outright or with a mortgage.[3]

Being the first branch meant that we developed modes of organising through practice. As a result, guidance is now available for newer branches that makes it easier for them to navigate the terrain. For example, the collective dispute model informs the way we identify common issues and address them together rather than providing individual support. Membership of the union is based on paying monthly dues and officials are elected at the Annual General Meeting (AGM). Members organise in individual branches that manage their own activities with support from those who work for the union. The Moss Side branch has monthly meetings, Know Your Rights sessions and its own AGM where officials are elected.

For the purposes of this chapter two African heritage members, Ekua and Thirza, talked to me about how most social housing tenants in the area were Black. The lack of diversity of the union's members, in terms of housing tenure and race, meant that many people's experiences of living in Moss Side were not being heard. Through door knocking, meeting people at the Know Your Rights sessions and conversations it became clear that social housing tenants faced major issues with their properties and broader issues in their lives. The neglect of many of the properties and the failure to address requests for repairs was a common story, as was the lack of sustained engagement with tenants. Similar patterns of neglect of rented properties mean that those living in the private rented sector faced major hazards.

It also became clear that tenants in Moss Side face many other issues. For example, many experience poverty through low-paid work and reliance on Universal Credit, exacerbated by the use of the sanction regime. This means that many fall into debt and/or rent arrears, which is an increasing experience as the impacts of Covid, the cost-of-living crisis and rising fuel costs have hit the poorest hardest. Covid led to school and workplace closures, which meant that many had no choice but to work or study from home. This created more pressure for those living in smaller houses or with limited resources and disproportionately impacted families living in working-class housing in places such as Moss Side. For Ekua and Thirza, these everyday experiences of their neighbours meant that their activism was broad-based and linked to the work of others in order to address the concerns that were being identified. An example of this broader partnership was the response to the hostile environment for asylum seekers and refugees. To bridge these different forms of resistance we established a partnership with Greater Manchester Law Centre and the Greater Manchester Immigration Aid Unit to set up a local Housing Justice network.

The membership fees do not cover the cost of the tenant organisers, therefore much of the activity of the Moss Side branch has been funded through grants from philanthropic or political organisations. For funding conditions, particularly for those grants secured before the principle of financial independence was adopted, we have inherited a legacy of expectations from the grant-makers. These include being asked to participate at national strategic level in policy-making and lobbying activity. The Greater Manchester focus on housing and homelessness, alongside the commitment to address racism in the provision of social housing and strategic housing services, has provided opportunities to take part in local policy-making and this may lead to the need to navigate competing demands.

These demands, and the tendency to engage in new campaigns in response to planned developments, such as the planned housing association investment in Moss Side and the development of purpose-built student accommodation, mean there has been little time to reflect on what we have learned about antiracist organising in the tenants' union and, more importantly, that this learning about becoming antiracist has not been shared with other branches yet. This means we need to build the capacity we need across Greater Manchester to ensure that an antiracist approach to building the tenants' union is adopted.

In reflecting on their activism, Ekua and Thirza discussed the way that changing housing is leading to the transformation of Moss Side. The loss of family housing is a consequence of the right to buy social housing policy, which saw millions of council houses being sold since the introduction of subsidies for tenants to buy them.[4] With nearly half of these houses found to be privately rented in 2015, the availability of affordable homes has been significantly reduced.[5] Landlords motivated by profit rent to those who will pay more, meaning students and Airbnb guests are increasingly living in what was family housing. Ekua explains how this is linked to proximity to the universities and the city centre, with the consequence for many residents that their children are unable to afford to live in the same neighbourhood:

> [W]e have lost so much family housing, and a lot of that has been the result of being able to buy your own house and then putting it out on the open market and then it being bought by landlords who are waiting to buy for student housing and Airbnb. There is a sense that we are part of the Oxford Road corridor that draws money into the city. As people living in the corridor we don't matter, our kids can grow up and not be able to live in the same community.

The combination of austerity and market-led housing provision reflects how the hostile environment has been extended to impact all our communities. Discussing the historic experience of new Commonwealth migrants in Moss Side, such as the Somali community who came in the 1990s and refugees arriving since 2000, Ekua explains the similarity of experiences across time: 'We can see our history being repeated for others. When people from Somalia arrived their housing need led to them being given social housing. As their children grow up here and they make Moss Side their home, we know that they will go through this same process of threat and attack.'

This transformation of the district means that social housing and the private rented sector increasingly meet the needs of new communities, becoming a 'transit zone' and reflecting provision for a mixture of those in acute need and the market. In turn this leads to the potential for significant tensions between these disparate residents brought together as neighbours with little state support to enable them to develop a shared sense of community. For the tenants' union this means that we need to have serious discussions about how we can contribute to building community and challenging the often dangerous and unaffordable conditions that people are living in.

Learning from History

The stigmatisation of Moss Side has a long history. Housing developments on agricultural land in the nineteenth century provided housing for the middle classes with larger houses and fresh air. The number of houses grew from fewer than 500 in 1861 to over 5,000 in 1901. The smaller terraces were developed in the early twentieth century. The area provided accommodation to support international trade, housing both embassies and visiting traders from Africa, Asia and Europe.[6] From the 1920s the larger houses were bought by landlords, who split them into multiple flats:

> The worst slums of Manchester are, however, not the two-up and two-down houses ... there are not enough of these houses ... and the surplus population is forced to overflow into houses

> let in lodgings ... [as] the pressure for housing accommodation increases ... [they] are let off to a number of families, generally one room to each family.[7]

The practice was called 'house farming' and led to concerns, not least because the rental costs were subsidised from the rates (the form of property tax at the time); in 1934, 20 per cent of the rates went on this (outdoor relief). There were also suspicions of collusion between tenants and landlords to claim the maximum rent allowable.[8]

The post-war migration from the Caribbean led to an increase in the population in Moss Side and Hulme, areas that were attractive because of the availability of employment, accommodation and lower levels of racial discrimination.[9] On their arrival, many moved into the neglected lodging houses and were often blamed by politicians for the conditions they lived in. The first places they lived were the run-down properties that the 'house farmers' had bought. Over time, using mortgage clubs and savings, around two-thirds of these families bought houses in the area.

Manchester developed plans to clear 'slum housing' in Moss Side and Hulme, replacing it with cities in the sky. The processes of slum clearance were lengthy, requiring a full survey of the area under consideration followed by a series of public and individual consultations before approval were signed off. This led to neglect and managed decline as the housing that people own has no value on the market, landlords will not maintain the properties and those tenants who could afford to do so moved elsewhere. Once the plans were agreed the council bought the properties using Compulsory Purchase Orders, which were not sufficient to allow the owners to buy similar property and led to many moving into social housing. To house the existing residents, new 'overspill' estates were built in satellite areas, many miles from the social and kinship networks that had developed.

Resistance by the newly formed Housing Action Group was built through public meetings, door knocking and a regular newsletter

Credit: Greater Manchester Tenants Union.

about ongoing events. *Moss Side News*[10] sold 1,500 copies through local newsagents and provided comprehensive coverage of the slum clearance, including the views of residents collected through the campaign. The first public meeting was attended by 500 people, and they raised a 3,000-signature petition calling for consultation and local resettlement. Over the next year they built the campaign through engaging with those facing clearance and publishing information on resettlement plans and what this would mean for people. This included advice on how to deal with the Compulsory Purchase Order procedure for owners and tenants. The local paper argued strongly for the community to participate in plans for the area and highlighted the problems with the solutions developed by the council: 'it is the experts who should be asking for permission to participate in the lives of the general public', 'Hulme was re-developed, was utterly destroyed ... hundreds of friendships and families scattered to different overspill estates', 'people in Hattersley who are living in damp homes far worse than any they are now pulling down and walking miles to a shop', and 'Just who is this city being rebuilt for?'

Their demand to contribute to the slum clearance plans reflected the recommendations of the national report *People and Planning: Report of the Committee on Public Participation in Planning*. The

Manchester Evening News condemned the failure of the council to follow the guidance from this report in their editorial in September 1969. Similar groups emerged in other parts of Manchester where slum clearances were being carried out and links were made with campaigns in other areas.

The insistence on consultation and willingness to publish their views on the council's activities led to a stand-off with the chief planning officer, who refused to come to talk to people in Moss Side. One local councillor described his own attitude to the Housing Action Group, though the three other elected members from a different party did condemn him:

> Moss Side Peoples' Association and Housing Action Group were run by nice people. They have been taken over by 'black power boys, parasites and stirrers' ... The council should help immigrants who want to go home by giving them a decent price for their houses so that they can pay their own fares. (Conservative councillor for Moss Side)

After the first few issues the Housing Action Group introduced a membership scheme and continued to report on the campaign for involvement in plans for the neighbourhood. Their reporting highlights how things would change with the redevelopment. One of the key demands was for accessible local shops. In the development plans the existing 500 corner shops were to be reduced to 50, many in the local district centre.

Many of the stories they covered echo contemporary struggles faced today. These include support from Manchester Students Union for Gypsies living on a derelict site near the university who faced eviction and a court order denying them access to any other sites in the city; a campaign to limit traffic and develop play streets; and an appeal to befriend older people in the clearance area who risked becoming isolated. *Moss Side News* also covered stories on racism and resistance in terms of policing in the area.

While *Moss Side News* reported on racism and resistance in terms of policing in Moss Side, and at least two of the three officers were well known Black activists, Kath Locke and Beresford Edwards, it did not provide explicit information about Black involvement in the struggles against slum clearance. We looked at *Black Voice*,[11] the paper of the Black Unity and Freedom Party, which involved members such as Kath Locke, to help us understand how the housing struggles were organised and the role taken by Black-led organisations. This provided further insights into the centrality of housing struggles to the activities of Black-led organisations. Our research showed that the housing struggle in Moss Side was inclusive, representing all residents of the areas under threat. *Black Voice* provided

Credit: Black Unity and Freedom.

powerful arguments and information from a working-class, antiracist perspective on both national and local struggles.

In the first edition, the main story argued that 'housing is a basic need. Everyone needs somewhere to live. It is essential for a good life. And just as everyone needs somewhere decent to live, so too everyone pays lip-service to this view. In practice, those who make the most noise about it always do the least to turn their words into deeds.' It explained that slums are sustained by capitalism, that government approaches to housing are racist and that there is an urgent need to address people's housing needs. The paper also had an article that explained tenant rights under the 1965 Rent Act and personal reflections on living in Moss Side:

> I will not argue that Moss Side is fairly tolerant and racism is not rife on the surface. But I will argue with people who say that racism does not exist because, having to live in concentrated poverty, we are all deprived. … for just under the surface it can be found in many subtle experiences of discrimination.

Black Voice continued to highlight housing issues and campaigns in London, Manchester and Liverpool. Articles, often provided by local activists, shed light on the issues of police brutality, racism in the workplace, racism in education and the disproportionate effects of the cost of living. Two key elements of their programme were the need for Black unity against racism and the importance of a class-based analysis.

The first slum clearances took place in the early 1970s, with people displaced into overspill estates and the focus of local activism moved onto the appalling conditions in the newly built housing in Hulme. In one of the last editions the Housing Action Group reported on the planned clearance of the second major tranche of housing, what was to become the Alexandra Park Estate. The plans showed that more than 2,500 families needed rehousing but fewer than a quarter would be accommodated within the local area.

In contrast, the later campaign against the clearance of the terraced housing on the other side of Princess Parkway was led by a community development worker on a project supervised by the local Anglican priest.[12] This campaign was much less inclusive, with only four from a survey of 60 households in 1972 being Black. Once the threat of clearance was lifted in 1975, the housing association, Moss Care, which he had set up with other local churches, began to acquire houses using funding from the Housing Corporation. By 1979 they were managing nearly 500 properties.

Our research on the history of struggles in Moss Side has revealed many stories of interest around the 5th Pan-African Congress in Manchester in 1945, the struggles against slum clearance in the 1960s and 1970s, and the experiences of Black people in policing and education at that time. This work has been used to secure funding for work with young people in Moss Side from the 81 Acts project to explore and interpret these archival resources on the experiences that led to the riots in Moss Side in 1981.

Lessons Learned

From our members' own experiences, our campaigning and our research into histories of resistance we reject liberal approaches informed by moral imperatives to help the 'deserving poor'. Inner-city districts in Manchester, such as Moss Side and Hulme, have a long history of housing interventions and resistance to the actions of the local state and developers. These historical perspectives create perspectives of place, for both those who live there and those who plan and shape the built environment.

We have experienced issues in our aspiration to develop an anti-racist tenants' union, and in reflecting on this we provide some further learning. Outside of the Moss Side branch people are less empowered to talk about racism, and those who do talk tend to put significant emotional labour into these conversations. For many members this means making themselves vulnerable and having to argue that they are worthy of support. Some have also internalised their oppression through dominant narratives about how racialised minorities get what they deserve. Our failure to spread the learning beyond the Moss Side branch reflects the increasingly demanding agenda created by worsening social conditions and the expectations of legacy funders. We expect this to worsen significantly with increasing homelessness among the refugee community, limited protection from eviction for tenants in the private sector and hazardous environments experienced by those living in the private sector and socially rented housing.

We argue that it is essential to work with tenants to improve their conditions, to create safe spaces to listen to their lived experience and, where appropriate, to develop campaigns that address common concerns. This informs our support for wider social justice campaigns seeking to address issues such as policing, education, culture and the hostile environment for migrants. We provide spaces to learn about wider struggles for the rights to the city in the UK and elsewhere. We consider and highlight strategies to address the challenges posed by changing populations and transformations designed to colonise local neighbourhoods by the city and its major institutions. We hope the lessons we are learning will inform the development of strong tenants' unions to support working-class and racialised communities living in social and private rented housing. Our planned activity for 2024 and beyond includes developing a list of publicly owned land in Moss Side to inform challenges to local planners and housing associations to build social housing to meet local needs and to organise Black members' events to spread the learning we have developed in Moss Side across Greater Manchester.

9

Breaking the Cycle:
Repairing Harms through
Climate Reparations

Tipping Point UK

Tipping Point UK understands the ongoing climate crisis as a product of colonial capitalism in which the state protects the perpetrators of planetary distress while impoverished and marginalised communities suffer disproportionately. Through our work we honour and learn from ancestors that resisted expropriation, extraction, enslavement, forced indenture, patriarchy and much more. Escalating climate change impacts carry the signature of systems that have for centuries enabled the capture of land and resources by elites. We carry the past and future in our peasant organising and in our collective visioning, building for collective well-being. We have been inspired by the Asian Peoples' Movement on Debt, Comité pour l'Abolition des Dettes illégitimes, Demand Climate Justice and the Climate Justice Now! Coalition. Our work is also informed by the outcomes of the National People of Color Environmental Leadership Summit (Washington, DC, 1991) and the World People's Conference on Climate Change and the Rights of Mother Earth (Bolivia, April 2010).

As a workers' cooperative committed to internal care policies, we support diverse movement ecosystems of resistance to climate chaos, resilience and alternatives. We support groups and networks capable of building collective power that can topple and replace our current oppressive economic, political, social and cultural systems. We come from diverse identity backgrounds, having held varying class positions and having experienced racialisation, migration, state violence, ableism, gender-based violence, homophobia, biphobia, transphobia and other marginalising forces. We disagree on a lot but are united in our conviction that by building community power we can reorient towards the radical changes necessary to ensure well-being. As Audre Lorde said, our differences need not separate us, they can spark creativity, connection and community for liberation.

We foster action and community while living in a time of multiple crises. Here in the UK, the rising cost of living is forcing people to choose between eating and heating their homes. Around the world, police and other state forces are killing young Black and Brown people with impunity, and assassinating or criminalising environmental and land defenders. And climate chaos is destroying homes and livelihoods. Climate change disproportionately hurts those least responsible for the increasingly formidable floods, storms, droughts, sea level rise and much more. These impacts further hurt those already living on the edge of survival, including women, younger and older people, people of colour, the disabled, LGBTQI communities, migrants, the stateless and Indigenous communities. And all while the rich are getting richer, profiting from people's suffering, and promoting and protecting the interests of banks and polluting corporations over people and the planet.

We aim to address the root causes of injustice to create people-powered climate justice and systems change. We believe that if enough people (i.e. around 3.5 per cent of the UK population) organise together, we can bring down the financial, legal, social and political pillars propping up fossil-fuelled capitalism. How we do things is as important as what we do.[1] We organise collectively, with care. We repair as we fight. We build places of rest, recovery, action and connection. Through this, we can build power beyond trauma, beyond the systems of pain we did not choose, and can, in our communities, redesign, reorganise and rebuild. We believe that by creating a powerful, nourishing and sustaining social 'tipping point' we can shift towards new post-extractive and care-based economic, political and cultural systems.

To create a 'tipping point', we support UK grassroots groups to build *critical connections* (depth) and *critical mass* (breadth). We use a three-point model for growing movement power:

- *Networks*: Growing and supporting grassroots networks. Given the scale of what must change so that we can live, no one organisation alone can win. We think systems change is only possible through collaborating in networks and sharing skills, resources and practices that work.
- *Momentum*: Building strategic cycles of mobilisation and absorption into the movement.
- *Action*: Enabling bold, sustained and creative community-led action.

We provide one-on-one tailored support to grassroots groups organising for all facets of social and climate justice. This support ranges from facilitating strategy sessions, to coordinated support for actions, to helping set up websites and mailing lists. We provide training on climate justice and climate reparations to groups focusing on migrant, racial, housing, land, trade unions and other forms of social justice, and training on intersectional justice to groups campaigning on climate change. We also connect groups to one another to stand in solidarity on issues they care about at regional gatherings across the UK.

We provide coordination support to three networks in the climate justice movement: the Climate Reparations Network, Stop Cambo/Rosebank and Defund Climate Chaos. The Climate Reparations Network focuses on demanding that polluters pay for loss and damage caused by climate change and fighting for a future rooted in reparative justice. The Stop Cambo/Rosebank network fights against fossil fuel projects in the UK; it successfully stopped the proposed Cambo oilfield from moving ahead and is now focused on stopping Rosebank, another proposed oilfield in the North Sea. Defund Climate Chaos demands that big banks and insurers stop funding the fossil fuel projects that are wrecking our climate.

We started organising as a small group in the lead-up to COP26 in Glasgow (2021) and we are now a team of 18 organisers working remotely and part-time. Some of us support groups according to location, for example the north-east or north-west of the UK, others according to thematic area of focus, for example Fossil Finance or Care and Repair. We think carefully about how we walk and have cultivated spaces to dream up visions of thriving movements.

Loss and Damage Youth Coalition

From flooding in Pakistan to drought in East Africa, communities around the world face the devastating impacts of climate change. Countries in the Global South did little to cause the climate crisis but are facing the sharp end of its impacts. Early industrialisers (such as the UK, other European countries, the USA and Australia) are disproportionately responsible for the emissions wreaking havoc. By 2030, it is estimated that the economic cost of loss and damage in the Global South will reach between US$290 billion and US$580 billion each year, and exceed US$1 trillion annually by 2050.[2] Families are witnessing the walls of their homes being ripped away during unprecedented storms in places such as Mozambique. Communities in eastern Africa experience cycles of drought and flooding resulting in hunger, displacement and more. Small islands and delta regions are losing land to rising sea levels. Drinking water is contaminated and salty sea water stops crops from growing. Unprecedentedly high temperatures across Asia affect global food supply chains while also impacting well-being.

The Loss and Damage Youth Coalition (LDYC) called for action and finance to address these injustices. LDYC has hundreds of members around the world, engaging in advocacy, training, storytelling, research and communications. In the lead-up to COP26 in Glasgow, we helped LDYC undertake strategic reflections, use our digital organising tools (Action Network) and bring youth delegates to Glasgow. LDYC continued this work in the lead-up to and during COP27, and we worked to connect them with influential social media storytellers and influencers. Some of their most active youth organisers have become country negotiators in the United Nations Framework Convention on Climate Change (UNFCCC). Through a recent partnership with the Climate Justice Resilience Fund, LDYC has established a grants programme that funds youth-led loss and damage initiatives on the ground. The partnership is the first ever grants programme for which grantee projects are selected entirely by a council of youth.

LDYC's advocacy, including open letters and other actions, have contributed to mainstreaming the demand for loss and damage finance with powerful videos that have reached millions on social media.

In a major win for climate justice advocates, during COP27 (Sharm El Sheikh, 2022) governments that are members of the UNFCCC agreed to establish a Loss and Damage Fund. At COP28 (Dubai, 2023) some countries began making contributions to the fund, although the current totals pledged fall far short of what is needed. In addition, the fund will be housed by the World Bank and there is a risk it will prioritise profit-making insurance over community-defined reparative justice.

In reflecting on what they've learned, LDYC members emphasise the importance of autonomy balanced with collective strategy, persistence, teamwork, powerful storytelling and advocacy by those most impacted. LDYC has also leveraged partnerships and networks to increase their impact. In addition to organisational collaboration, they emphasise that it's vital to be kind to one another, having regular check-ins and caring on a personal level for each other's well-being.

From a Tipping Point UK perspective, we have enjoyed weaving connections across movement spaces to the benefit of LDYC, and making our tech tools available to them. Our systemic analysis of injustices pre-empted that the loss and damage climate finance fund agreed at COP28 would fall short of systemic justice demands. Yet we also believe that the networks formed will both hold the fund to account and continue to agitate for community centred reparative justice. We trust that in doing so, climate activists have begun committing to ideas of systems change beyond climate finance that reinforces neoliberal market dominance.

Stop the Silvertown Tunnel Coalition

The Stop the Silvertown Tunnel Coalition is a community-led group campaigning to stop the Silvertown Tunnel. It includes local parents, residents, climate activists, Green and Labour Party members, National Education Union members and others.

At the time of writing, the building work is, unfortunately, well underway for the Silvertown Tunnel. It will run under the Thames between Greenwich and Newham. It will have two lanes in each direction, half of which will be reserved for heavy goods vehicles under existing plans. The contract to build, manage and maintain it is held by the Riverlinx Consortium, which is made up of six companies: Aberdeen Standard Investments, BAM PPP PGGM, Cintra, Macquarie Capital and SK E&C.

Experts estimate that increased traffic from the tunnel will take London's carbon emissions above the limit required for the UK to meet its commitments according to the Paris Accord. It will also increase air pollution in Newham and Greenwich. The tunnel's feeder roads pass through residential areas and past several schools, directing new traffic towards them. Newham, home to City Airport, is already consistently found to be one of the most polluted local authorities in the UK. Exposure to high levels of air pollution can cause a variety of adverse health outcomes, for example it increases the risk of respiratory infections, heart disease and lung cancer. Newham is also the second poorest borough in London and 73 per cent of its residents are people of colour and half are migrants. In Newham and in the communities in the Global South on the front line of the climate crisis, the impact of the Silvertown Tunnel will be disproportionately felt by working-class people of colour.

The Stop the Silvertown Tunnel Coalition achieved too many things in 2021–3 to cover here, so instead we focus on one more experimental area: our attempts to target the Riverlinx Consortium, in particular Macquarie Capital. Although ultimately unsuccessful, we believe it is a useful strategic example.

In October 2021, we organised actions connecting activists and enabling global solidarity in recognition of the racialised exposure of air pollution from the geopolitical South through to impoverished parts of London. Then, in June 2022, we shared an open letter to the British LGBT Awards asking them to drop their co-headline sponsor Macquarie Capital. This letter drew attention to the environmental racism of the Silvertown Tunnel and the incompatibility of environmental racism and LGBT liberation. It also highlighted Macquarie Capital's involvement in the Rio Grande liquid natural gas project in Texas, which threatens sacred Indigenous historical sites of the Carrizo Comecrudo Tribe, and the Adani Coal mine in Australia, which is destroying the ancestral lands and waters of the Wangan and Jagalingou Traditional Owners. The letter was signed by more than 40 community groups, including Black Lives Matter UK, Lesbians and Gays Support the Migrants (LGSM) and Greenpeace UK. It was produced in consultation with groups in Texas and Australia and LGSM.

In June 2023, Macquarie Capital remained a co-headline sponsor of the British LGBT Awards, alongside new sponsors BP, HSBC and BNP Paribas. In April 2023, Tipping Point organisers held a workshop on the intersection of queer liberation and climate justice with Fossil Free Pride, a grassroots group that campaigns for prides across the UK to pledge not to accept sponsorship from fossil fuel companies, banks or investors. With support from Tipping Point, Fossil Free Pride held a protest outside the British LGBT Awards with testimony from front-line communities harmed by the award's sponsors, including the South-South and Triangular Cooperation (SSTC), East African Crude Oil Pipeline (EACOP) and the West Cumbria Mine. Drag kings and queens and DJs from Queer House Party performed. The awards dropped Shell and BNP Paribas immediately, and Fossil Free Pride are now in negotiations with them.

The focus of the campaign now is to repurpose the tunnel for cargo bikes, cycling and electric buses.

Three lessons stand out. First, health and air pollution has emerged as one of the most salient and unifying themes of the campaign, and as the tunnel goes ahead this will only become more important. Second, more work is needed to bring working-class Black and Brown communities, especially on the Newham side of the river, into the campaign. Third, when we connect intersecting struggles, such as LGBTQ liberation, trade unionism and climate justice globally, we create the potential for broad coalitions; building trust between movements takes time and an open letter is just a first step. Focusing on financial institutions can be a way to bring intersecting struggles together.

Recently, coalition members have bought air pollution monitors and held workshops on how to set them up. These are being placed at key locations in the community, such as primary schools. Coalition members are also teaming up with the London Renters Union Newham and Leytonstone Branch for community organising training and to talk about collaborations.

You can find the SSTC at @silvertowntn on X and www.stopsilvertowntn.com and Fossil Free Pride at @FossilFreePride on X and Instagram and www.fossilfreepride.co.uk.

Climate Reparations Network

The demand for climate reparations recognises that climate change is a result of colonisers' disproportionate pollution, extraction, exploitation and oppression.[3] The most polluting countries are relatively protected from the impacts of climate change, and the wealth extracted from people and land in the Global South has left those least responsible for emissions most exposed to climate change.[4] Colonialism and slavery justified the plunder of people and places. Relationships of interdependence and collective ways of being were replaced with domination and subjugation. This has continued through modern economic relationships of trade, investment and indebtedness.[5]

Climate reparations must include transfers of wealth from polluting countries and companies to the people in the Global South most affected by loss and damage. But reparations are not just about writing a cheque; they require a process of addressing the economic, political, social and cultural injustices that make some people more vulnerable to disasters than others. We must transform our societies to repair the harms caused by extraction and exploitation, to transition away from fossil-fuelled capitalism towards a world based on care and repair.

In 2021, Tipping Point and Platform London helped grassroots groups and activists come together to form the Climate Reparations Network. The network is made up of groups from around the UK that focus on many related struggles, including housing, migrant, health, land and racial and climate justice. We put together a series of 'stop and start' demands that outline our vision for the future: the government must stop funding fossil fuel projects and implementing hostile migration policies. It must start paying for climate harms and democratising renewable energy, banks, housing and public infrastructure.[6]

We have also collaborated with Makan to provide educational workshops about the links between climate injustice and apartheid in the Occupied Palestinian Territories. Following Israel's entrenchment of genocide in late 2023, we increased our collaboration with Makan to host climate justice power hours, giving hundreds of people the opportunity to target entities such as Barclays. Barclays holds over £1 billion in shares and provides over £3 billion in loans and underwriting to nine companies whose weapons, components and military technology have been used in Israel's genocide against the Palestinians. Barclays is also the biggest funder of fossil fuels in the UK.

We are working to concretise the Network's vision, purpose and structure so that we can continue to respond to members' needs and steward the Network in line with collective visions. These visions are disparate. We want to continue to resist while we also build counter-power. We see possibilities for community assets and wealth that generate wind, solar and hydro power while also regenerating and nourishing movement space for sustained community power constantly agitating towards systems change.

Climate Violence and State Violence

Tipping Point UK has built connections with organisations fighting environmental injustices, especially communities of colour that live close to hazardous industries and infrastructures in the northeast of England and London. We are also expanding the connections between different aspects of our work by targeting the banks and insurance companies that are funding and securing the fossil fuel industry and those profiting from our deadly border industry. We also understand the deep connections between the state oppression of Black communities and communities of colour and those actively resisting our unjust systems. One way this work has been supported by Tipping Point has been in relation to the activism that followed Chris Kaba's death.

Chris Kaba, an unarmed Black man, was shot and killed by a Metropolitan Police officer in September 2022 in Streatham Hill, South London. Chris was 24 years old and expecting a baby with his partner.

In the days following Chris's killing, we worked with members of the Climate Reparations Network to create an open letter from the climate justice movement in solidarity with Chris Kaba's family. It was signed by over 1,500 people and groups from Just Stop Oil to Climate Camp Scotland and Save Latin Village.

In November 2022, we held a vigil for Chris Kaba before the start of the Climate Justice Coalition's march in central London. The vigil included singing by the Nawi Collective and speeches from the Kaba family, the All African Women's Group and Revoke. At the end of the vigil a large canvas artwork featuring a portrait of Chris Kaba and the words 'Climate justice is racial justice' and 'Justice for Chris Kaba' was unveiled and carried into the Climate Justice Coalition march. This artwork, alongside others, connected white supremacy in East Africa to racism in South London, emphasising the need for international solidarity across the climate justice movement.

At the time of writing the IOPC investigation into the killing of Chris Kaba is still underway. We will keep organising in the climate movement in solidarity with the Kaba family.

Stop East African Crude Oil Pipeline

For us in Uganda, land is not just a factor of production, it is part of our natural and cultural heritage, it is life.

Diana Nabiruma

French oil company Total and the majority state-owned China National Offshore Oil Corporation are on the cusp of building the world's longest heated oil pipeline right through the heart of East Africa. Stretching for nearly 1,445 kilometres, the EACOP would have disastrous consequences for local communities, for wildlife and for the entire planet. The project threatens to displace thousands of families and farmers from their land. It poses significant risks to water resources and wetlands in both Uganda and Tanzania – including the Lake Victoria basin, which over 40 million people rely upon for drinking water and food production. The pipeline would also rip through numerous sensitive biodiversity hotspots and risk significantly degrading several nature reserves that are crucial to the preservation of threatened elephant, lion and chimpanzee species.[7]

When communities in these territories first learned about the plans for this project, they reached out to groups and communities facing similar struggles in Ecuador and Nigeria. Learning from each other and our shared struggles is necessary to stop giant projects such as the EACOP. Communities in East Africa realised they needed to build a powerful and creative movement that could resist the destruction and exploitation created by the EACOP. They first spoke with many organisations and collectives across their communities, including church leaders, regional partners especially in

Congo, other civil society groups around the world, groups taking governments to court and those challenging financial institutions. They then started the #StopEACOP campaign formed by groups and communities across Africa and the world.

After years of organising they have managed to create a coalition and have learned that coalition building is key in their struggle. The #Working in coalition with comrades from around the world creates a safety net for groups on the ground, giving them time to rest and repair when they need it. In this process they have realised intersections of their struggles and the importance of connecting the local with the global struggles.

Post-extractive Futures

We first convened a Post-extractivist Futures meeting in 2021, exploring the challenges in creating internationalist, global, just, equitable and powerful movements that listen to each other and move together. Weaver Participants came together in virtual spaces of conversation and art. We spoke of choosing life as a sign of emancipatory change outside of any pre-established formula and dogma of how to do things, of the need to braid ideas and feelings for futures beyond extractivism, decolonial, Indigenous, feminist, abolitionist futures, and so we became many more in an interweaving of affection and reciprocity.

The climate crisis universalises the existential pain that colonialism set us on a trajectory towards. But the past is playful. It can – in the realities and memory of front-line and Indigenous communities – also guide us to alternatives that have not yet been quashed. In this process, we are called to a multidimensional relationship with theory – drawing from past and present resistors of state violence, capitalism, racism, patriarchy, heteronormativity and ableism, and also from ancestral wisdom and the knowledge of ecosystems. We create plural cosmologies: north stars to guide us as we take care, move and act, ecologically recognising cycles and enabling us to be coherent with the kind of transformations we want. We play with approaches for change, drawing from art and dance as much as from movement theories of change. In attempting to start as we hope to continue, we offer a creative piece:

We feel the contradictions between the pessimisms of reason and the hopes of the spirit.

There are lives that no longer exist, that resist.

Colonial capitalism is sinking in its own disaster and it will fall. We trust. It breaks through like a bulldozer, extracting and sucking, stiffening our capacity to wonder and to care for ourselves, to imagine plural ways of thinking about a better life for all, with the Earth.

With no qualms about the questions of tenderness, these clumsy and lifeless systems burst forth, impregnating emotions with the thought of fear, fear of otherness. All systems and dynamics that the machine embraces encourage exhaustion (ruptures of cycles), separation (of body/soul/spirit, or humans with other-than-human beings, of elements), supremacy (hierarchies between diversities), and violence.

In its face, we move in the midst of imposed dualities. However, certainly we know that fear, competition, striving, all this is a tiny region of our soul. We are far more than dominant systems allow, especially systems that allow for little.

With deep love, surprise, gratitude, sweetness and joy, we are going through a moment of profound changes towards other possible worlds. Visions of worlds where human beings are medicine to ecosystems, and vice versa.

The ancestors tuck us in, we carry them in our life forces. They help us to sustain hurts in a world where life is a privilege. We are displaced by wars, by the pains of processes of rupture, violence, suffering and permanent emergency. Although we come striving for personal experiences, we look with astonished eyes at the light of new births, the re-encounter with art, to the rhythm of the voices of territories resisting and vibrating.

Lessons for the Future

Organising around climate reparations has helped us to imagine worlds where all people and the planet live well, without domination, extraction or exploitation. By identifying white supremacy, colonialism and capitalism as the root cause of the climate crisis, the call for climate reparations invites both social justice activists outside of the climate movement and climate activists working outside of a social justice framework into this act of radical imagination.

In coming together, we remember that the past and present unfolds differently in our many spaces of interconnection. Our differences do not separate us, we join for life and dignity and are inspired by Colombian movement calls for unity ('juntanza'). Yet our remembering and interconnecting is necessarily imperfect. We are limited by speaking the languages of colonisers, and often in connecting through virtual spaces where we are separated by time zones and cannot feel the physicality of movements we seek to nourish us. We struggle against the tide of (some) movement funders that do not see the work of cultivating grassroots community-led power as fundable work. We struggle against our own demons that tell us we are imposters in this work, that we are not doing enough. We struggle in the many contradictions. Yet by dancing and listening to each other at our collective rhythm, we welcome contradictions. We continue to take time to build relationships and to do so with care, to foster trust across differences as a constant action. We walk on roots that smell of honey, wet soil, the aroma of fruits impregnated in the skin under the sun and trees, of flavours to be discovered. *We walk slowly to walk safely.*

10
We Have Nothing to Lose but Our Chains

Sisters Uncut

Dedicated to Megan – our Sister forever.

> I will come to my Sisters
> not dutiful,
> I will come strong.
>
> Pat Parker, 'Womenslaughter'

Sisters Uncut is an abolitionist, feminist direct action movement in the UK. Founded in late 2014 to protest cuts to domestic abuse services, we have since turned our attention to building liberatory alternatives that intervene in and disrupt state violence. Our politics are founded on Black feminist principles: that the state is also a perpetrator, as violent to women as our partners are; and that although all women can experience domestic violence, our ability to escape and survive is determined by the intersection of race, class, immigration status and disability. We recognise the irrevocable connection between the private and public spheres, and the way the state colludes with individual perpetrators to enact and create the conditions for coercion, control and violence. This is why we resist the violence of colonisation, policing, border regimes and prison systems.

When we came together, two women a week were being killed by a partner or ex-partner.[1] Domestic violence services were subjected to outsourcing: 'service providers' were forced to undercut each other for contracts with statutory funders and run services on a shoestring. Refuge doors were closing on women escaping violence. After decades of professionalisation, as well as increasingly close links to carceral systems, the Violence Against Women and Girls (VAWG) sector had severed its connection to the militant, self-organised refuge movement of the 1970s[2] and was almost entirely dependent on state funding. Organisations were reluctant to challenge the ravages of austerity for fear of biting the hand that fed them. Much of the sector was hostile to trans and gender non-conforming people. It was hostile to sex workers and unable to provide effective specialist support to women of colour, disabled folk and those living with addiction. This was amplified by the scarcity culture that austerity instilled: specialist services that supported women with 'complex' needs (homelessness, criminalisation, substance use and mental health issues) were being undercut by cheaper generalist providers.

Sisters Uncut stepped into the political arena, demanding that services be fully funded so all women could safely flee abuse. We fought for an inclusive, intersectional feminism in which all experiences of gendered violence would be given weight, respect and solidarity and in which all survivors would be supported, with particular attention on the most marginalised. With this in mind, our focus over the last decade has shifted from domestic abuse services to resisting state violence more broadly – tackling not just central government budgeting but housing, prisons and police violence. Our organising tactics have varied between mass mobilisation, longer-term local community organising and coalition building.

Between our first meeting and finalising this chapter in 2024, life in Britain has undergone significant shifts, with a virulent reactionary nationalism building on the austerity regime imposed since 2010. The interim period has delivered dramatic cuts to public services, the Brexit referendum, the rise and fall of Boris Johnson, the Covid-19 pandemic and a massive deterioration in our living conditions. Of course, these same years bore witness to the sweet shock of Jeremy Corbyn's election as Labour Party leader, the 2020 Black Lives Matter uprisings, the 2021 Kill the Bill movement that followed the murder of Sarah Everard and the emergence of abolitionist politics into the mainstream. These shifting political sands have informed our tactics, as well as our targets, over the last nine years, from media stunts to squatting prison buildings, from storming council meetings to setting up CopWatch groups.

Our journey over the last decade has also been propelled by the relationships we built in the process; being part of Sisters Uncut changed us. Through organising together, we've felt our own inner worlds expand and our ideas about community deepen. We also felt the pain of failure, the hopelessness of political defeat and the turmoil of group conflict. Nonetheless, sisterhood is powerful, and that power has spilled into the rest of our lives. Sisters are trade unionists, housing organisers, prison abolitionists, climate campaigners and more: we haven't stopped organising, even during times when the group has been inactive.

Here, we revisit our early years of organising together and identify some of the defining moments in the development of our abolitionist praxis. Although it is by no means a complete account of the organising and mobilising of Sisters across the country, we reflect on working in coalition and using diverse tactics to build power against racialised and gendered violence, and conclude with our thoughts on what's next for feminist organising.

Early Years: Making Headlines as a Single Group

Between 2015 and 2016, we made our name taking direct action that was disruptive and beautiful, with a razor-sharp media strategy. The Sisters Uncut action strategy was inspired by anti-austerity campaign UK Uncut, and their formula of 'issue, target, tactic, hook'. When planning actions, we'd agree on the issue, who we'd target, what tactic we'd use and, crucially, what external event we'd hook it to in order to make it newsworthy. Once we'd decided this, we split into working groups with specific responsibilities to plan and deliver the action: logistics, media, propaganda and outreach, each element slotting together on the day.

We knew our actions could leave no room for interpretation. We poured red dye in the Trafalgar Square fountains to symbolise the blood of women killed by partners; we held a mass funeral to memorialise refuges that had been forced to close; we jumped on to the red carpet at the *Suffragette* film premiere, highlighting that 'dead women can't vote'; we burned copies of the *Daily Mail* outside their head office, connecting our activism to traditions of Black feminism; and we blockaded the doors to the Treasury in the days running up to another eye-watering austerity budget.

In a left-wing landscape still dominated by men in anoraks holding Socialist Worker placards, the burst of colour and energy from Sisters Uncut charmed the press. The irony that the objectification of women landed a group of militant feminists into newspapers wasn't lost on us – we understood our influence would come from building a media narrative that connected the deaths of women with central government decision-making. We produced clear press releases with our own photography and developed a shrewd knack of befriending journalists. The *Telegraph* and *Daily Mail* reproduced our messages verbatim. It's no coincidence that, between 2015 and 2016, then Chancellor George Osborne felt compelled to once again include domestic abuse provisions in his budget announcements.[3] We made careful use of social media, controlling our own narrative and how our collective was represented.

We have always held solidarity and collective struggle at the heart of our organising strategy and political principles. Shortly after we formed, Sisters Uncut actively began supporting the efforts of other groups and campaigns; from these relationships our own politics developed. It has been critical for us to show up for others, to use our strength in the service of community and to ensure we leave no one behind. In 2015 we regularly joined the Movement for Justice demonstrations outside Yarl's Wood immigration detention centre in Bedfordshire. At this time, the exposure of the appalling physical and sexual violence experienced by women caged in Yarl's Wood highlighted the fact that violence against women happens wherever women are stripped of their power, from police cells, to prisons, to immigration detention.

To this day, we continue to support the annual United Friends and Families Campaign (UFFC) march to remember those killed by the

Dying Trafalgar Square fountains red in November 2015 (Guen Murroni)

Blockading the Treasury in March 2016 (Claudia Moroni)

state and to amplify their tireless campaigns for justice and accountability. Every year we join the rally in solidarity with those left
behind in grief: the leaders of UFFC, who are mostly the mothers,
aunts, sisters and daughters of murdered Black men, reminding us
that racialised, gendered violence has many faces. Although our
focus is on harm perpetrated against women and non-binary folk,
ignoring the experiences of men (especially Black and other racialised men) at the hands of the state was never an option. Police exist
to maintain the status quo and keep capitalist society functioning for
the elite. It is no wonder that both cops who kill Black people and
men who kill women rarely, if ever, face justice: the justice of capitalism was never designed to protect us.

Our solidarity with other groups strengthened the bonds between
us too. Our weekly Thursday night meetings became an anchor for
many of us: in fun, messy and complicated ways we found belonging with each other. We did our best to cultivate care through a
'safer spaces' policy that we read out at the start of every meeting.
It encouraged us to reflect on our individual positionality and what
we were bringing into the group, to be willing to learn and accept
critique, and crucially to 'create the change we wish to see in the
world'. Our group aimed to be non-hierarchical; we alternated
the facilitator role every week and made decisions by consensus
which – although requiring lengthy discussions, disagreement and
compromise – guided us towards actions we could all support. Consensus also had its downfalls. Strict consensus processes enable any
individual to 'block' a proposed decision from going ahead. At one
meeting in 2015, our original plan to dye the Trafalgar Square fountains red, which was supported by around 40 people, was blocked
by a newcomer to the group who was concerned that dye was not
animal friendly.

Our infrastructure was nurtured by an ethos of sharing labour
between subgroups, for example finding and booking meeting
spaces, ensuring we had funds for travel costs and protest materials,
training each other in facilitation and media skills, and coordinat-
ing social events around childcare. Beyond the organising work, we

formed friendships, partied together and found love, demonstrating how organising can create a platform for radical community building. While it has been a life-affirming experience, our community and trust in one another was also tested with interpersonal and ideological conflicts, social anxiety, burnout and heartbreak.

A notable test happened in Portsmouth in December 2015. Sisters in London had been working alongside VAWG sector workers in the City who'd contacted us when they found out about proposed sweeping cuts to the vital services where they worked.[4] Portsmouth Sisters Uncut formed in response, and after several meetings they planned an action targeting the Portsmouth Full Council meeting to draw public attention to the cuts and make the council's proposal politically untenable. We corralled journalists and staged a 'die-in' outside Portsmouth Guildhall to retain our focus on victims and disrupted the council meeting by dropping a large banner and letting off party cannons containing 4,745 pieces of confetti, each symbolising a phone call reporting domestic abuse in the city the previous year.

For the first time, a Sister was arrested during the action. We had always planned actions to avoid arrests. Although she was later released into the arms of those waiting outside, this was a cautionary moment for the group. As a result we spent time working on our approach to internal accountability: how should we address harm caused by our own actions in a way that enables us to grow and develop as a community where no one is disposable? We didn't answer that question right away, but in developing our transformative justice toolkit we began to turn our abolitionist principles into practical organising tools. Portsmouth taught us that creative, joyful and media-savvy actions would not always protect us from the force of the state. We would be violently reminded of this lesson several years later, when police attacked our vigil at Clapham Common following the murder of Sarah Everard.

Our central organising group averaged around 40 people in 2015–16. But as our actions drew more members, it became increasingly challenging to find an accessible central London meeting space and to make decisions through consensus. In late 2015, after we jumped onto the red carpet and landed in front of the world's media, we had upwards of a hundred Sisters attending meetings and our organising structures started to creak. How could we start our meetings with a go-round if that alone would take up half of the meeting? How could we balance our commitment to movement building with anxieties around state surveillance and infiltration? How could we tackle issues in our local communities when all meetings were in central London? Around 18 months after we formed, in early 2016, we decided to review our organising tactics and political priorities.

Growth: The Transition to Regional and Neighbourhood Organising

Forced by practicality as much as our evolving politics, we took steps to move into smaller groups based on geographies. With such large numbers we were able to shift towards building power in our communities. It was at this level we saw the potential to wrestle liberation from the hands of elites by building grassroots power, as opposed to appealing to the sensibilities of national politicians through the spectacle of media stunts. We wanted to win tangible change for our neighbours and communities and for the women in them experiencing violence.

We set about a series of negotiations on how a Sisters Uncut 'DNA' should be defined, from our position on trans inclusion and anti-carceral principles to our logos and colours. We wanted to ensure individual groups had autonomy while being part of an ideologically and visibly connected movement. Eventually, the core London group became three: East, North and South-East. Before and after the London split we expanded into cities across the UK, including Doncaster, Portsmouth, Leeds, Birmingham, Bristol, Edinburgh, Glasgow, Manchester and Cardiff. Our work, ideas and networks were growing.

East End Sisters Uncut were quick to respond to the gendered and racialised effects of gentrification in Hackney. We kicked off community organising with weekly street stalls on Ridley Road Market in Hackney, London. We engaged Saturday shoppers on Hackney issues, inviting them to a nearby meeting. The conversations and meetings were invaluable as a forum through which the number of empty council flats in Hackney was highlighted by Hackney residents. After some research, we connected with temporary accommodation residents placed on a hollowed-out council estate due for demolition: Marian Court.

Typical of contemporary regeneration programmes, the plan was to cut the number of council flats on-site, to increase the units for sale or shared ownership. Combining our demand for domestic violence services with the demands of Marian Court residents for safe, accessible and secure housing, we layered direct action, negotiation and administrative pressure in a Summer of Action.

Paying homage to the birth of the refuge movement, we reclaimed an empty flat on Marian Court by squatting it, turning it into a women's space for the summer of 2016. This served as a base to escalate tactics and build local support for our demands, while gaining local and national publicity. Hosting breakfast clubs, communal dinners, sports days, crèches and political workshops, the reclamation brought a community of people together around a shared struggle for women's safety, affordable housing and public space.

Nine solid weeks in a physical space expanded our organising capacity in manifold ways compared to the weekly meetings and online messaging we did previously. Many Marian Court residents had been placed in temporary accommodation on the estate after being made homeless due to domestic violence or racist hate crimes. Naturally, conversations were drawn towards the links between gendered, state and racist street violence. Points of solidarity between Marian Court, wider Hackney residents and Sisters Uncut members visiting from across the city and country expanded our political vision enormously.

With the regeneration programme now well under way, Marian Court has been reduced to rubble. When our space closed in September 2016, one resident hoped we could one day make a mural or plaque to commemorate our struggle. By writing down our memories, we hope to keep the embers burning until that day. We also recognise that the legacy of the Marian Court women's space endures in other ways. Some of the residents and homeless survivors that organised or took shelter there have since taken up roles as full-time community housing organisers and domestic violence workers in the wider movement for safe homes and communities.

To achieve tangible results it is crucial to establish solidarity between community members, become experts in local authority decision-making practices and statutory duties, and develop a dogged commitment to uncovering data about local issues councils hope to obscure.

In 2016, Sisters Uncut North London turned their attention to HMP Holloway, the notorious women's prison. We rose up in grief at the news of Sarah Reed's death and organised a vigil and teach-out outside the prison in April 2016, to grieve, show solidarity with Sarah's family and make it clear that the state was the perpetrator.

Sarah died in Holloway after suffering years of neglect, abuse and violence at the hands of the state. In the days leading up to her death, she was denied medication and kept from seeing her family and lawyers. Sarah was incarcerated in 2015, charged with grievous bodily harm after defending herself against a serious sexual assault while detained in Maudsley Hospital. Several years earlier, she had been violently assaulted by a male Metropolitan Police officer, an incident caught on camera. The neglect and cruelty she suffered is exemplified by an incident that followed the death of her newborn baby in hospital; Sarah was given her child's body and told to take it for burial herself. Sarah's experiences of state violence highlight the overlapping and pernicious violence many Black women experience. Her story showed that the state we had been petitioning was itself a perpetrator of racist and sexist violence; that gendered and racialised state violence are symbiotic.

The vigil was North London Sisters Uncut's first action and would begin a long-term relationship with the site of HMP Holloway. In late 2015, it had been announced that the prison was going to close.[5] Holloway's closure marked the acceleration of a prison expansion strategy in England and Wales as it was successively announced that 10,000 new prison units would be built,[6] including five 'community prisons' specifically for women.[7] It was clear to us that the state's priority was to expand its web of violence rather than provide support to those at risk; that new prisons were going to be a key mechanism of intensified social control during the ensuing period of socio-economic crisis. After our vigil for Sarah, North London Sisters Uncut joined Reclaim Holloway, a coalition of local groups concerned about the closure. Reclaim Holloway was campaigning for the site to be used for the benefit of the community; as the land was public the coalition believed it should be used for public good. Our demands included social housing and a building that could provide support and community space for women and non-binary people who had experienced domestic, sexual and/or state violence.

In the following summer of 2017, North London Sisters Uncut occupied the Visitor's Centre on the recently closed prison site. In an act of reclamation, they took over the building for a week-long Community Festival. Like our comrades before us in Marian Court, we reclaimed the building to create a beautiful space where we cooked communal meals and hosted a schedule of activities and political workshops on a range of issues.

As a result of the community campaign and the occupation, our demand for a Women's Building was included in the council's planning requirements for the site. However, in 2023 we resisted proposed plans for the site which would significantly diminish the community vision for public land for public good. The Holloway campaign vividly spotlights how systems of oppression coagulate in the prison as a form of punishment and control. The vision of the campaign paints a picture of what abolition could look like: to reclaim land that has been used to oppress and transform it in the interests of our collective liberation.

Abolition in the Mainstream: Sarah Everard and Kill the Bill (2021)

In March of 2021, still deep in the coronavirus pandemic, the UK was confronted by the horrific kidnapping and murder of Sarah Everard in South London. Despite our deep knowledge of police violence, many of us were still shocked to find out that a serving Metropolitan Police officer, Wayne Couzens, was responsible. Couzens was known within the police force as a violent man and sexual predator; he was given the nickname 'The Rapist' by his colleagues. As much as they tried to focus the narrative on Couzens as a single 'bad apple', it was impossible for policing as an institution to avoid the spotlight: the Metropolitan Police incubated, protected and empowered him, giving him guns, a warrant card and the power to act with impunity despite the many signs of his violent character.

A small group, organising under the banner of Reclaim These Streets, called a vigil for Sarah, only to retract their call at the behest of the same police force guilty of her murder. Doing the bidding of one of the UK's most draconian home secretaries, the police used Covid legislation to criminalise protest and our right to occupy public space. Although many Sisters groups had slowed down in the years between 2018 and 2021, Sisters were willing and ready to step in to host the vigil. We weren't alone, thousands of people came to grieve together that night on Clapham Common. What happened at the vigil is well documented, and social media was awash with images of police officers, drunk on power, storming the park's bandstand and violently dragging women through the park. Sarah Everard's vigil was twisted into a further site of gendered and state violence.

The following week in March 2021 would mark the government's first attempt to pass the Police Crime Sentencing and Courts (PCSC) Bill: a pernicious piece of legislation that massively extended police powers, curbed the right to protest and targeted already over-policed communities. Despite its reach, the legislation had received little attention from activists and media alike. After the police violence at the vigil, Sisters Uncut declared 'we need to kill this bill' and the Sisters Uncut media machine seized the opportunity to present the scenes at Clapham Common as a harbinger of how the draconian legislation would be enforced. We called another action outside Scotland Yard the very next day.

Over the next few weeks, with comrades up and down the country, we called demonstrations under the banner of Kill the Bill (KTB). Hundreds of thousands of people took to the streets over several weeks, we delivered online training to empower communities to set up local KTB groups, we spoke on the radio and we appeared on broadcast news, taking abolitionist ideas into mainstream media. We launched the KTB coalition with other activists, organisations and community groups most affected by the PCSC Bill, which provided the infrastructure for another year of action. This moment was significant, marking the return of grassroots solidarity and coalitionism in left-wing politics. From Black youth groups, sex workers and Gypsy, Roma and Traveller communities to trade unionists, feminists and environmental activists, we were all under one banner, united against a piece of legislation that violently targeted us all.

The movement saw some early success, bringing groups across the country together, sparking huge protests (the largest of which saw more than 10,000 people on the streets during the pandemic) and even forcing the Labour opposition to vote against the bill despite their initial intention to abstain. The Tories' 80-seat majority gave them legislatory carte blanche, and they were able to push much of the bill through the Commons and eventually (despite some hard-won resistance) the Lords. Sisters had recognised early on that, like our elders who resisted the Poll Tax, we had to beat the bill through mass action and street resistance. Unfortunately, we failed to win this argument in the coalition, and when the bill inevitably passed, demoralisation and defeatism set in, splintering bonds and cementing political differences. We learned that without a clear, shared understanding of the political terrain, coalitional bonds can be fragile.

Nonetheless, our decisive action to reframe Sarah Everard's murder as political, to connect police violence at the vigil to the bill and to insist that police brutality is systemic rather than the result of 'bad apples' has made a long-term impact. It is at least part of the reason why the police continue to face a crisis that shows no signs of abating. The Casey Report, Cressida Dick's eventual resignation and the exposure of 'policing by consent' as a malicious fiction were propelled by our incisive narrative and the efforts of a broad-base coalition.

For Sisters, the ongoing crisis of authority is also an opportunity to argue for the dismantling of the criminal justice system. This means making real the promise of abolition, by building alternative models of care and resisting state violence through solidarity, mutual aid and ungovernability. This was demonstrated in our series of 'Raise the Alarm' actions between November 2021 and March 2022, when hundreds of women and femmes confronted police-perpetrated misogyny and sexual violence by loudly hand delivering a complaint to the Royal Courts of Justice and then setting off a thousand rape alarms outside a central London police station renowned for its violent and dismissive treatment of survivors.

Our learning from the KTB coalition cements the crucial role of strong connections with comrades across the radical left; it means strategising to resist the erosion of our right to protest; it means working with and through difference, turning solidarity from abstraction to praxis; and it means building communities of care to sustain our movement during a time of defeat, uncertainty and political apathy writ large.

Mass Movements Start in Communities: Tactics for Building Power

Sisters believe that organising in our communities is at the heart of building the mass movement we need in order to secure our collective liberation. Our regional groups expanded our membership exponentially, and we were able to tackle local as well as national issues with more capacity and reach. Our contribution to building the CopWatch Network, as the KTB movement slowed down, has further highlighted the value of building local networks and has also helped us learn about operating reactively as well as through traditional regular meetings, caucuses and events. Tackling national and international issues is informed by conversations with our neighbours and from the alternatives we test on our doorsteps.

Given the increasingly violent landscape of gendered violence, and the attacks on our right to protest, our earlier stunt tactics are no longer enough by themselves. When we came together in grief for Sarah Everard and were met with appalling police violence, we were reminded of the imperative to educate ourselves and others about building alternatives to the dead ends of carcerality and capitalism. Although the creativity, joy and connection created by our direct actions is still very much needed, our modes of protest and dissent must deepen in readiness for the issues and opportunities ahead.

Sisters have created a huge number of resources, which are all published on our website and freely available for anyone to use. Suggested tactics to build feminist abolition in your community include:

- Poster and sticker campaigns.
- Weekly stalls sharing information, food and invitations to get involved.
- Regular public meetings.
- Social events and hangouts.
- Police intervention and know your rights training.
- Direct police intervention and street patrols.
- Workshops and talks.
- 'Subvertising' campaigns on public transport systems.
- Banner- and placard-making sessions.
- Mutual aid and community care groups.
- Breakfast clubs and food sharing.
- Building coalitions and solidarity with other local groups.
- Arrestee support (for your own and other actions).
- 'Thinking spaces' and other talking circles.
- Fun days.
- Football tournaments and sports days.
- Social media networks, groups and blog posts.
- Multiple forms of protest, such as divestment campaigns, boycotts, sit-ins and occupations.

We always learned as we went along and believe fiercely in the power of collective political education to develop our tactics and our principles together. In writing this, it's clear how agile we need to be in the face of an enemy as powerful as the state. Our relationships and communities are the source of courage, replenishment and care from which we will build and hone the tools we need to do this.

What's Next for Feminist Organising?

The terrain of feminist organising in the UK has shifted significantly since Sisters Uncut first formed. In this moment, our early struggles to safeguard state-funded services seem worlds away from our now dedicated abolitionist organising. That struggle to safeguard is far from over and austerity is ramping up as the UK economy flails under the continued global crisis of capitalism – feminists must remain vigilant to the threat of cuts to vital services and public infrastructure. Our struggles must continue to attack the systemic foundations of gendered violence and oppression, taking aim at the ideologies, institutions and actors that abuse, incarcerate and murder us.

It is painful to all of us that, at a time of rampant attacks on our physical and material safety, much-needed political energy is being expended on slowing the spread of violence incited by so-called gender critical feminists, or as they are known to us 'trans-exclusionary radical feminists'. We do not recognise the divisions they seek to forge between us, and we do not recognise their reductive and essentialist concept of gender. All Sisters groups have been targeted by transphobes at some stage during our work, but since 2017, Sisters in Edinburgh have worked in coalition with other groups to publicly resist the spread of transphobic violence and hatred in Scotland, supported and perpetrated by state institutions and mainstream political parties as well as community groups and local media. Stuart Hall, describing the mainstream media characterisation of Black men in the turbulent 1970s, would undoubtedly look on trans people as one of the 'folk devils' of contemporary British society. In a global landscape of increasing violence, crisis and disaster, solidarity between all women, indeed with and between all working-class people, has never been more crucial to our collective survival and liberation. We know that until our trans siblings are safe on the streets, in their homes and in our institutions, none of us are.

Sisters Uncut was founded to organise at the intersection of violence and safety, to demand accountability for funding cuts, to highlight state violence within the immigration system and to call for action against police and prison violence that has killed and harmed our siblings. In the wake of Sarah Everard's murder, there is growing popular acknowledgement that systemic misogyny and racism ensures that not only do the police fail to keep women safe, they actively brutalise and murder us. In the wake of the scathing Casey Report, abolitionist-feminist demands can no longer be dismissed as the views of a radical minority. Feminist organising now poses a significant threat to the already weakened credibility of police and criminal justice agencies.

In such a hostile and violent political context, we must resist attempts to divide and distract us. Coming together in solidarity and coalition, Sisters can build networks of care and justice in our neighbourhoods, on our streets and in state institutions. In the words of Assata Shakur, 'we have nothing to lose but our chains'.

Notes

Introduction

1. This massive transfer of wealth from the public to private and corporate landlords is driving the housing crisis; 2022–3 data estimate the cost at £17 billion annually. https://england.shelter.org.uk/media/press_release/homeless_accommodation_bill_hits_17bn_.

2. Refugee Action, 2023, 'Hostile Accommodation: How the Housing Asylum System Is Cruel by Design', www.refugee-action.org.uk/wp-content/uploads/2023/03/Hostile-Accommodation-Refugee-Action-report.pdf.

3. 'A New Feminist Offensive, Interview with Aviah Sarah Day', 2023, *The Political Leap: Communist Strategy Today* 19 (Notes from Below).

4. Tabatha Vaughn, 2021, 'The Radicalism of "Race Today"', *Tribune*, https://tribunemag.co.uk/2021/08/beyond-journalism-the-radicalism-of-race-today.

5. Arun Kundnani, 2020, 'What Is Racial Capitalism?', www.kundnani.org/what-is-racial-capitalism/.

6. Satnam Virdee, 2014, *Race, Class and the Racialised Outsider*, London: Bloomsbury.

7. Jonas Marvin, 2021, 'Brexit from Below: Nation, Race and Class', *Salvage* 10 (The Disorder of the Future).

8. Aamna Mohdin, 2020, 'Legal Threat over Anti-capitalist Guidance for Schools in England', *The Guardian*, 1 October, www.theguardian.com/education/2020/oct/01/legal-threat-governments-anti-capitalist-guidance-schools-political.

9. Olivia Williams, 2011, 'London Riots: Is Twitter to Blame?', *Huffpost*, 8 October, www.huffingtonpost.co.uk/2011/08/08/london-riots-twitter-that_n_920791.html.

10. Adam Elliott-Cooper, Phil Hubbary and Loretta Lees, 2020, 'Moving beyond Marcuse: Gentrification, Displacement and the Violence of Un-homing', *Progress in Human Geography* 44(3): 492–509.

11. Cedric Johnson, 2023, 'Police Exist to Manage and Contain Surplus Populations', *Jacobin Magazine*, https://jacobin.com/2023/04/police-exist-to-manage-and-contain-the-surplus-population.

12. *The Guardian*, 2011, '2011: The Year in Review', 30 December, www.theguardian.com/uk/2011/dec/30/2011-end-of-year-review.

13. Kareem Fahim, 2011, 'Slap to a Man's Pride Set off Tumult in Tunisia', *New York Times*, 21 January, www.nytimes.com/2011/01/22/world/africa/22sidi.html?_r=1&pagewanted=2&src=twrhp.

14. Torres, L., Munoz, M., Warren, T., Kameräde, D., Beck, V. Fuertes, V., Magnus, L., and Morris, C., 2023, 'Underemployment Levels and Trends: Time, Skills, and Wages', The Underemployment Project, https://trends.underemployment.info/.

15. Michael Denning, 2010, 'Wageless Life', *New Left Review* 66 (November–December).

16. Karl Marx, 1993, *Grundrisse: Foundations of the Critiques of Political Economy*, London: Penguin Classics, emphasis in original.

17. Ian Shaw and Marv Waterstone, 2021, 'A Planet of Surplus Life: Building Worlds beyond Capitalism', *Antipode* 53(6), https://doi.org/10.1111/anti.12741.

18. Fred Hampton, 1969, *We Have to Protect Our Leaders*, speech delivered at the Capitol Theater, 19 May.

19. A. Harnecker, 2015, *A World to Win: New Paths toward Twenty-First Century Socialism*, New York: Monthly Review Press, 167.

20. G. Wilder, 2009, 'Untimely Vision: Aime Cesaire, Decolonisation, Utopia', *Public Culture* 21(1): 105.

21. Harnecker, *A World to Win*, 25.

22. V. Bevins, 2023, *If We Burn: The Mass Protest Decade and the Missing Revolution*, London: Hachette.

23. Harnecker, *A World to Win*, 14.

24. UN Mauritius, 2021, 'International Day for the Remembrance of the Slave Trade and Its Abolition: A Date, a Symbol, a Vision and a Monument', https://mauritius.un.org/en/142274-international-day-remembrance-slave-trade-and-its-abolition-date-symbol-vision-and-monument.

25. See Peter Linebaugh and Marcus Rediker, 2000, *The Many-Headed Hydra: The Hidden History of the Revolutionary Atlantic*, London: Verso; Julius Scott, 2018, *Common Winds: Afro-American Currents in the Age of the Haitian Revolution*, London: Verso.

Chapter 1

1. No More Exclusions member, roundtable, 2022.

2. Bernard Coard, 1971, *How the West Indian Child Is Made Educationally Sub-normal in the British School System*, London: New Beacon Books; Lyttanya Shannon (dir.), 2021, *Subnormal: A British Scandal*, Rogan Productions.

3. Brian Richardson (ed.), 2005, *Tell It Like It Is: How Our Schools Fail Black Children*, London: Bookmarks Publications; George Padmore Institute, 1965–88, 'The Black Education Movement (Early Period), 1965–1988', https://catalogue.georgepadmoreinstitute.org/records/BEM.

4. Kehinde Andrews, 2013, *Resisting Racism: Race, Inequality, and the Black Supplementary School Movement*, London: Institute of Education Press; Heidi Safia Mirza and Diane Reay, 2000, 'Spaces and Places of Black Educational Desire: Rethinking Black Supplementary Schools as a New Social Movement', *Sociology* 34(3): 521–44; Beverly Bryan, Stella Dadzie and Suzanne Scafe, 2018, *Heart of the Race: Black Women's Lives in Britain*, London: Verso.

5. Hazel Carby, 1982, 'Schooling in Babylon', in Centre for Contemporary Cultural Studies (ed.), *The Empire Strikes Back: Race and Racism in 1970s Britain*, London: Hutchinson & Co., 181.

6. Paulo Freire, 2018, *Pedagogy of the Oppressed*, New York: Bloomsbury Academic.

7. Angela Davis, 2003, *Are Prisons Obsolete?* New York: Seven Stories Press, 38–9.

8. Zahra Bei, Helen Knowler and Jabeer Butt, 2021, 'How Do We Progress Racial Justice in Education? School Exclusion, Systemic Racism and Off-rolling', *IPPR Progressive Review*: 122–42; Megan Whitehouse, 2022, 'Illegal School Exclusion in English Education Policy', *Emotional and Behavioural Difficulties* 27(3): 220–30.

9. Department for Education, 2023, 'Suspensions and Permanent Exclusions in England', https://explore-education-statistics.service.gov.uk/find-statistics/suspensions-and-permanent-exclusions-in-england#.

10. We use the term 'global majority' to acknowledge that Black people, Indigenous people and people of colour represent a majority of the world's population. This term emphasises our shared experiences and struggles and recognises our collective power.

11. Zahra Bei, 2020, 'When Will Disabled Black Lives Matter?', ALLFIE, 27 November, www.allfie.org.uk/news/blog/when-will-disabled-black-lives-matter/; Subini Ancy Annamma, 2018, *The Pedagogy of Pathologization: Dis/abled Girls of Color in the School–Prison Nexus*, New York: Routledge.

12. Eleanor Busby, 2020, 'Pupil Repeatedly Sent Home from School over Afro Hair Wins £8,500 Payout', *The Independent*, 11 February, www.independent.co.uk/news/education/education-news/afro-hair-discrimation-student-legal-action-payout-ruby-williams-urswick-school-a9323466.html; Equality and Human Rights Commission, n.d.,

'Ruby Williams vs Urswick School', https://legal.equalityhumanrights. com/en/case/stopping-school-using-discriminatory-hairstyle-policy.

13. Angry Workers, 2022, 'An Interview on the Pimlico Spring', 20 April, www. angryworkers.org/2022/04/20/an-interview-on-the-pimlico-spring/.

14. Adam Elliott-Copper, 2021, *Black Resistance to British Policing*, Manchester: Manchester University Press; Jessica Perera, 2020, 'How Black Working-Class Youth Are Criminalised and Excluded in the English School System', Institute of Race Relations, https://irr.org.uk/wp-content/uploads/2020/09/How-Black-Working-Class-Youth-are-Criminalised-and-Excluded-in-the-English-School-System.pdf; Laura Connelly, Roxy Legane, and Remi Joseph-Salisbury, 2020, 'Decriminalise the Classroom: A Community Response to Police in Greater Manchester's Schools', Kids of Colour and Northern Police Monitoring Project, https://nopoliceinschools.co.uk/resources/Decriminalise%20the%20Classroom%20-%20A%20Community%20Response%20to%20Police%20in%20Greater%20Manchester%27s%20Schools.pdf; Remi Joseph-Salisbury and Derron Wallace, 2021, 'How, Still, Is the Black Caribbean Child Made Educationally Subnormal in the English School System?', *Ethnic and Racial Studies* 45(8): 1426–52; Karen Graham, 2014, 'Does School Prepare Men for Prison?', *Analysis of Urban Change, Theory, Action* 18(6): 824–36.

15. Just for Kids Law, 2020, 'Excluded, Exploited, Forgotten: Childhood Criminal Exploitation and School Exclusions', www.justforkidslaw.org/sites/default/files/fields/download/JfKL%20school%20exclusion%20and%20CCE_0.pdf.

16. Cabinet Office, 2017, 'Race Disparity Audit: Summary Findings from the Ethnicity Facts and Figures Website', www.ethnicity-facts-figures.service.gov.uk/static/race-disparity-audit-summary-findings.pdf.

17. Ministry of Justice, 2012, 'Prisoners' Childhood and Family Backgrounds: Results from the Surveying Prisoner Crime Reduction (SPCR) Longitudinal Cohort Study of Prisoners', www.gov.uk/government/publications/prisoners-childhood-and-family-backgrounds.

18. Ministry of Justice and Dominic Raab MP, 2021, 'New Prison Strategy to Rehabilitate Offenders and Cut Crime', www.gov.uk/government/news/new-prison-strategy-to-rehabilitate-offenders-and-cut-crime; T. J. Coati, n.d., 'What's Wrong with Secure Schools?', *Abolitionist Futures*, https://abolitionistfutures.com/latest-news/whats-wrong-with-secure-schools#:~:text=For%20them%2C%20the%20fact%20that,of%20child%20imprisonment%2C%20means%20they.

19. Cradle Community, 2021, *Brick by Brick: How We Build a World Without Prisons*, London: Hajar Press; Roxy Legane, 2022, 'The Manchester Ten

and the Injustice of "Conspiracy" Charges', *Red Pepper*, 23 September, www.redpepper.org.uk/society/race-racism/the-manchester-ten/.

20. Jaden Moodie Movement, 2020, 'Jadens Law: A Halt to School Exclusions until a Suitable Alternative Education Is Given', Change.org, 25 August, www.change.org/p/department-of-education-jadens-law-a-halt-to-school-exclusions-until-a-suitable-alternative-education-is-given.

21. Beverly Bryan, Stella Dadzie and Suzanne Scafe, 2018, *Heart of the Race: Black Women's Lives in Britain*, London: Verso Books, 238.

22. Charlene Carruthers, 2019, *Unapologetic: A Black, Queer, and Feminist Mandate for Radical Movements*, Boston: Beacon Press.

23. Combahee River Collective, 1977, *Combahee River Collective Statement*, www.blackpast.org/african-american-history/combahee-river-collective-statement-1977/.

24. Audre Lorde, 2007, *Sister Outsider: Essays and Speeches*, Berkeley: Ten Speed Press.

25. Kennetta Hammond Perry, 2022, 'Black Futures Not Yet Lost: Imagining Black British Abolitionism', *South Atlantic Quarterly*, July: 541–60.

26. No More Exclusions, n.d., 'What About the Other 29? And Other FAQs', https://drive.google.com/file/d/15JxRG5jgsDCoq-T2gJFmLHv VdA5EPYFk/view.

27. No More Exclusions, 'What About the Other 29?'.

28. Virgie Hoban, 2021, '"Discredit, Disrupt, and Destroy": FBI Records Acquired by the Library Reveal Violent Surveillance of Black Leaders, Civil Rights Organizations', Berkeley University of California, www.lib.berkeley.edu/about/news/fbi; Rob Evans, 2018, 'Police Spies Infiltrated UK Leftwing Groups for Decades', *The Guardian*, 15 October, www.theguardian.com/uk-news/2018/oct/15/undercover-police-spies-infiltrated-uk-leftwing-groups-for-decades.

29. No More Exclusions, 2021, 'Why We Need a Moratorium on School Exclusions', https://drive.google.com/file/d/1bNni9VaqqMHsWKDPf dYWVoDwZMl2qbEc/view.

30. Liberty, Art Against Knives, No More Exclusions, Northern Police Monitoring Project, Joint Enterprise Not Guilty by Association, Release, INQUEST, National Survivor User Network, Maslaha and Kids of Colour, 2023, 'Holding Our Own: A Guide to Non-policing Solutions to Serious Youth Violence', www.libertyhumanrights.org.uk/fundamental/holding-our-own-a-guide-to-non-policing-solutions-to-serious-youth-violence/.

31. Alex Johnston and Latifa Akay, n.d., 'Radical Safeguarding: A Social Justice Workbook for Safeguarding Practitioners', Maslaha, www.maslaha.org/Project/radical-safeguarding.

32. No More Exclusions, 'What About the Other 29?'.

33. Richard Adams, 2022, 'Teachers Say They No Longer Want Police Based in Schools after Child Q Outrage', *The Guardian*, 1 April, www.theguardian.com/education/2022/apr/11/teachers-say-they-no-longer-want-police-based-in-schools-after-child-q-outrage.

34. Nadine White, 2022, 'Europe's Largest Teachers Union NEU Hit with Racism Allegations by Its Own Members', *The Independent*, 12 April, www.independent.co.uk/news/uk/home-news/neu-teaching-union-racism-allegations-b2054156.html.

35. Charlie Spencer, 2020, 'Serious Case Review: Tashaûn Aird (Child C)', City of London and Hackney Safeguarding Children Partnership, December 2020, https://chscp.org.uk/wp-content/uploads/2022/07/CHSCP-SCR-Tashaun-Aird-Child-C-Report-PUBLISHED-FINAL2.pdf.

36. No More Exclusions member, roundtable 2022.

Chapter 2

1. Research undertaken for this chapter related to the history of resistance to racist policing in Manchester was supported by the Arts and Humanities Research Council (AHRC) [AH/V006673/1].

2. T. Chowdhury, 2017, 'Watching the Cops: The Genesis of the Northern Police Monitoring Project', *Justice, Power and Resistance* 1(2): 308–15.

3. Chowdhury, 'Watching the Cops'.

4. M. Busteed, 1997, 'The Irish in Nineteenth Century Manchester', *Irish Studies Review* 5(18): 8–13; J. Jenkinson, 1988, 'The Black Community of Salford and Hull 1919–21', *Immigrants & Minorities* 7(2): 166–83.

5. R. Makonnen, 2017, *Pan-Africanism from Within*, Diasporic Africa Press, 143; Michael Herbert, 1992, *Never Counted Out! The Story of Len Johnson, Manchester's Black Boxing Hero and Communist*, Manchester: Dropped Aitches; Shirin Hirsch and Geoff Brown, 2023, 'Breaking the "Colour Bar": Len Johnson, Manchester and Anti-racism', *Race & Class* 64(3): 36–58.

6. Christopher Fevre, 2021, '"Race" and Resistance to Policing before the "Windrush Years": The Colonial Defence Committee and the Liverpool "Race Riots" of 1948', *Twentieth Century British History* 32(1): 1–23.

7. L. Connelly, 2022, 'The Police Cannot Keep Us Safe: Violence against Women and Institutional Misogyny', in NPMP (ed.), *Reflections and Resistance: NPMP Magazine 2022*, http://npolicemonitor.co.uk/blog/.

8. J. Gilmore and W. Tufail, 2013, 'Police Corruption and Community Resistance', *Criminal Justice Matters* 94(1): 8–9.

9. Chowdhury, 'Watching the Cops'.

10. Gilmore and Tufail, 'Police Corruption and Community Resistance'.
11. nopoliceinschools.co.uk.
12. Active from 2018 to 2022, Resistance Lab was a coalition of activists, tech and data experts, community members and researchers, which sought to combine education, technology and research to better highlight how state violence impacts upon marginalised communities. See: resistancelab.network.
13. Resistance Lab, 2020, *A Growing Threat to Life: Taser Usage by Greater Manchester Police*, resistancelab.network/taser-report.
14. See: http://npolicemonitor.co.uk/uncategorized/police-pursuits-we-must-kill-the-bill/ and http://npolicemonitor.co.uk/uncategorized/statement-on-record-high-number-of-road-traffic-deaths-involving-greater-manchester-police/.
15. nopoliceinschools,co.uk; NHS, n.d., https://transform.england.nhs.uk/information-governance/guidance/sharing-information-with-the-police/.
16. P. Williams and E. Kind, 2019, *Data Driven Policing: The Hardwiring of Discriminatory Policing Practices across Europe*, Brussels: European Network Against Racism.
17. NPMP, 2022, 'Statement on Record High Number of Road Traffic Deaths Involving Greater Manchester Police', http://npolicemonitor.co.uk/uncategorized/statement-on-record-high-number-of-road-traffic-deaths-involving-greater-manchester-police/.
18. https://nopoliceinschools.co.uk/resources/Decriminalise%20the%20Classroom%20-%20A%20Community%20Response%20to%20Police%20in%20Greater%20Manchester%27s%20Schools.pdf.
19. http://npolicemonitor.co.uk/blog/.
20. B. Clarke, K. Chadwick and P. Williams, 2017, 'Sites of Resistance: Reflections on Relationships, Power and Positionality', *Justice, Power and Resistance* 1(2): 261–82.
21. https://irr.org.uk/person/siva/.
22. S. Grover, 2020, 'In Memory of A. Sivanandan, the Director Emeritus of the Institute of Race Relations', The Monitoring Group, https://tmg-uk.org/publications/blog-post-title-two-p7lh5.
23. K. Blowe, 2022, *Local Police Monitoring: A Practical Guide*, London: Netpol, 4.
24. See: S. Harris, R. Joseph-Salisbury, P. Williams and L. White, 2021, 'A Threat to Public Safety: Policing, Racism and the Covid-19 Pandemic', Institute of Race Relations, https://irr.org.uk/wp-content/uploads/2021/09/A-threat-to-public-safety-v3.pdf.
25. Blowe, *Local Police Monitoring*, 4.

26. https://jacobin.com/2021/07/andre-gorz-non-reformist-reforms-revolution-political-theory.

27. This concept is drawn from the US Black Panther Party. See, Huey Newton, 1972, *To Die for the People: The Writings of Huey P. Newton*, New York: Random House, 104.

28. G. M. Bradley and L. de Noronha, 2022, *Against Borders*, London: Verso.

29. R. Joseph-Salisbury and L. Connelly, 2019, 'Macpherson, Twenty Years on: Diversifying the Police Won't End Institutional Racism', NPMP, http://npolicemonitor.co.uk/blog-grid-homepage/long-read-macpherson-twenty-years-on-diversifying-the-police-wont-end-institutional-racism/.

30. www.manchestereveningnews.co.uk/news/greater-manchester-news/manchester-council-quietly-scraps-mayors-21101498; https://themeteor.org/2021/07/20/manchester-school-based-police-officers/#:~:text=Manchester%20city%20council%20has%20decided,public%20attention%20to%20the%20issue.

31. www.manchestereveningnews.co.uk/news/greater-manchester-news/manchester-council-quietly-scraps-mayors-21101498.

32. https://truthout.org/articles/police-reforms-you-should-always-oppose/.

33. Runnymede Trust, 2023, 'Over-policed and Underprotected: The Road to Safer Schools', www.runnymedetrust.org/publications/over-policed-and-under-protected-the-road-to-safer-schools.

34. Stuart Hall, 1996, 'New Ethnicities', in David Morley and Kuan-Hsing Chen (eds), *Stuart Hall: Critical Dialogues in Cultural Studies*, London: Routledge, 445.

35. https://archive.nytimes.com/opinionator.blogs.nytimes.com/2015/12/10/bell-hooks-buddhism-the-beats-and-loving-blackness/.

36. Claire Alexander and Will Shankley, 2020, 'Ethnic Inequalities in the State Education System in England', in Bridget Byrne, Claire Alexander, Omar Khan, James Nazroo and Will Shankley (eds), *Ethnicity, Race and Inequality in the UK: State of the Nation*, Bristol: Policy Press.

37. Nazia Parveen, Niamh McIntyre and Tobi Thomas, 2021, 'UK Police Forces Deploy 683 Officers in Schools with Some Poorer Areas Targeted', *The Guardian*, 25 March; Laura Connelly, Roxy Legane and Remi Joseph-Salisbury, 2020, *Decriminalise the Classroom: A Community Response to Police in Greater Manchester's Schools*, Manchester: Kids of Colour and Northern Police Monitoring Project, 18–19.

38. Resistance Lab, 2020, *A Growing Threat to Life: Taser Usage by Greater Manchester Police*, Manchester: Resistance Lab.

39. NPMP, n.d., 'Statement on Record High Number of Road Traffic Deaths Involving Greater Manchester Police', http://npolicemonitor. co.uk/uncategorized/statement-on-record-high-number-of-road-traffic-deaths-involving-greater-manchester-police/.

40. For example, see Janet Batsleer, 1988, 'The Viraj Mendis Defence Campaign: Struggles and Experiences of Sanctuary', *Critical Social Policy* 8(22): 72–9; and Eddie Abrahams, 1989, 'Citizenship and Rights: The Deportation of Viraj Mendis', *Critical Social Policy* 9(26): 107–11.

41. Manchester's Radical History, 2011, 'Gus John and the Moss Side Defence Committee', 1 October, https://radicalmanchester.wordpress. com/2011/10/01/gus-john-and-the-moss-side-defence-committee/.

42. For a good example of NPMP's individual and collective writing on histories of resistance see the 2022 issue of our magazine, *Reflections and Resistance*: http://npolicemonitor.co.uk/blog/.

43. Amy Hall, 2022, 'Beyond Punishment', *New Internationalist* 536 (March–April), 18.

44. Randall Williams, 2003, 'A State of Permanent Exception: The Birth of Modern Policing in Colonial Capitalism', *Interventions* 5(3): 322–44. Also, see Aviah Sarah Day and Shanice Octavia McBean, 2022, *Abolition Revolution*, London: Pluto Press, 106–12.

45. Tanzil Chowdhury, 2021, 'From the Colony to the Metropole: Race, Policing and the Colonial Boomerang', in Koshka Duff and Cat Sims (eds), *Abolishing the Police*, Dog Section Press, 85.

46. Simon Peplow, 2019, *Race and Riots in Thatcher's Britain*, Manchester: Manchester University Press, 167–8.

47. Jasbinder S. Nijjar, 2018, 'Echoes of Empire: Excavating the Colonial Roots of Britain's "War on Gangs"', *Social Justice* 45(2–3): 147–62, 149. Also, see Adam Elliott-Cooper, 2021, *Black Resistance to British Policing*, Manchester: Manchester University Press, esp. chapter 5.

48. Nijjar, 'Echoes of Empire', 155.

49. Patrick Williams and Becky Clarke, 2016, *Dangerous Associations: Joint Enterprise, Gangs and Racism: An Analysis of the Processes of Criminalisation of Black, Asian and Minority Ethnic Individuals*, London: Centre for Crime and Justice Studies; 2018, Amnesty International UK, *Trapped in the Matrix: Secrecy, stigma, and Bias in the Met's Gangs Database*, London: Amnesty International UK.

50. For a critical primer on these surveillance technologies, see Patrick Williams and Eric Kind, 2019, *Data-Driven Policing: The Hardwiring of Discriminatory Policing Practices across Europe*, Brussels: Open Society Foundations, 14.

51. NPMP, n.d., 'Statement on the Unjust and Racist Prosecution of 10 Boys in Manchester', http://npolicemonitor.co.uk/uncategorized/

statement-on-the-unjust-and-racist-prosecution-of-10-boys-in-manchester/; Selam Gebrekidan, 2022, 'They Called Him a Gangster out for Revenge: The Evidence? 6 Text Messages', *New York Times* (International Edition), 16 November.

52. Northern Police Monitoring Project, 2022, 'On Manchester Caribbean Carnival Entry Refusals', July, http://npolicemonitor.co.uk/uncategorized/on-manchester-caribbean-carnival-entry-refusals/.

53. Moya Lothian-McLean, 2022, 'Black People Nearly Eight Times More Likely to Be Banned from Manchester Carnival', *Novara Media*, 5 October, https://novaramedia.com/2022/10/05/black-people-nearly-eight-times-more-likely-to-be-banned-from-manchester-carnival/.

54. A. Mohdin, 2023, 'Manchester Police Stop Carnival Bans after Legal Threat over "Racist Targeting"', *The Guardian*, 4 August, www.theguardian.com/uk-news/2023/aug/04/manchester-police-ban-gangs-carnival-legal-threat.

55. www.lse.ac.uk/justice-equity-technology/Justice-Equity-and-Technology-Table.

56. R. D. G. Kelly, 2002, *Freedom Dreams: The Black Radical Imagination*, Boston: Beacon Press.

57. A. Y. Davis, 2005, *Abolition Democracy: Beyond Empire, Prisons, and Torture*, New York: Seven Stories Press.

58. www.maslaha.org/Project/Radical-safeguarding.

59. L. Lock, 2022, 'Why Are We Still Pretending This Police Watchdog Is Independent?', *Novara Media*, https://novaramedia.com/2022/11/21/why-are-we-still-pretending-this-police-watchdog-is-independent/.

60. See: https://peoples-tribunal.org/.

Chapter 3

1. Filipa César, 2019, 'Meteorisations: Reading Amílcar Cabral's Agronomy of Liberation', Buala, www.buala.org/en/afroscreen/meteorisations-reading-amilcar-cabral-s-agronomy-of-liberation.

2. https://landforthemany.uk/.

3. Food Matters, 2023, 'The Sankofa Report: British Colonialism and the UK food system', www.foodmatters.org/wp-content/uploads/2023/03/Sankofa-final.pdf.

4. Charles W. Mills, 2017, *Black Rights/White Wrongs: The Critique of Racial Liberalism*, Oxford: Oxford University Press.

5. Guy Shrubsole, 2019, *Who Owns England? How We Lost Our Green and Pleasant Land, and How to Take It Back*, London: HarperCollins.

6. Corinne Fowler, 2020, *Green Unpleasant Land: Creative Responses to Rural England's Colonial Connections*, Leeds: Peepal Tree Press Ltd;

Nick Hayes, 2020, *The Book of Trespass: Crossing the Lines That Divide Us*, London: Bloomsbury.

7. Legacies of British Slavery Project, University College London, www.ucl.ac.uk/lbs/.

8. Eric Williams, 2021, *Capitalism and Slavery*, 3rd ed., Chapel Hill: University of North Carolina Press.

9. Josina Calliste, 2021, 'This Land Is Our Land', *New Economy Zine* 4, https://neweconomics.org/uploads/files/NEFZINE-issue4-WEB-FINAL_2021-11-03-135755.pdf.

10. Josina Calliste, Sam Sivapragasam and Marcus McDonald, 2021, 'Rootz Into Food Growing: Uplifting Black and Racialised Growers in London', https://static1.squarespace.com/static/5eeceooee6780d38b9fb012f/t/60ace24b8b87b828f51ec72e/1621942864883/FINAL+Rootz+into+Food+Growing+report+25.05.21.pdf.

11. Naomi Terry, 2023, 'Jumping Fences: Land, Food and Racial Justice in Britain', https://static1.squarespace.com/static/5eeceooee6780d38 b9fb012f/t/63b599ddb28c5936edc62cff/1672845804758/Jumping+Fences+2023+Web.pdf.

12. CARICOM (Caribbean Community) is an intergovernmental organisation and political and economic union made up of 15 member states.

13. *The Alternative*, 2022, 'What if artists rehearsed a life-affirming economy? Though everything from sci-fi gardens to artist-supporting hotels, Birmingham's MAIA shows how', 9 November, www.thealternative.org.uk/dailyalternative/2022/11/14/what-if-artists-rehearsed-a-life-affirming-economy.

14. Oxford Real Farming, 2023, 'How Do Prisons and Policing Impact and Intersect with Our Struggles for Land Justice', YouTube, www.youtube.com/watch?v=06L1Di9u2Lo&ab_channel=OxfordRealFarming.

15. Shrubsole, *Who Owns England?*

16. Anita Sethi, 2022, 'Kinder Scout 90 Years on: UK's National Parks Still Largely White and Middle Class', *The Guardian*, 24 April, www.theguardian.com/travel/2022/apr/24/kinder-scout-90-years-on-uks-national-parks-still-largely-white-and-middle-class.

17. Bernice Johnson Reagon, 1983, *Coalition Politics: Turning the Century in Home Girls – A Black Feminist Anthology*, edited by Barbara Smith, Kitchen Table Press, 356–68, https://womenwhatistobedone.files.wordpress.com/2013/09/1983-home-girls-coalition-politics-bernice-johnson-reagon.pdf

18. Olúfẹ́mi O. Táíwò, 2022, *Reconsidering Reparations*, Oxford: Oxford University Press, 74.

Chapter 4

1. See Akram Salhab, 2023, 'Stitching Together the Threads of Internationalism: London in Anti-imperial Organising', *Race and Class* 65(1), https://journals.sagepub.com/doi/full/10.1177/0306396 823116690.
2. For an engaged recent academic discussion of internationalism see D. Dirik, M. Younis, M. Chehonadskih, L. Uddin and M. Davidson, 2023, 'The Meanings of Internationalism: A Collective Discussion on Pan-African, Early Soviet, Islamic Socialist and Kurdish Internationalisms across the 20th Century', *Millenium: Journal of International Studies*, https://doi.org/10.1177/03058298231175700.
3. Workers in Palestine, n.d., 'An Urgent Call from Palestinian Trade Unions: End all Complicity, Stop Arming Israel', www.workers inpalestine.org/the-calls-languages/english.
4. The Non-Aligned Movement was a group of Third Worldlist states that sought to build a power bloc in the international order tied to neither the United States or the USSR.

Chapter 5

1. Awate Suleiman (@AWATEMUSIC), 'Today, "go back to Africa" becomes government policy. It's also 5 years since 72 people lost their lives in the preventable tragedy of Grenfell. When will this Hostile Environment end?' Twitter, 24 June 2022.
2. Luke de Noronha, 2019, 'Deportation, Racism and Multi-status Britain: Immigration Control and the Production of Race in the Present', *Ethnic and Racial Studies* 42(14): 2413–30.
3. Gracie Mae Bradley and Luke de Noronha, 2022, *Against Borders: The Case for Abolition*, La Vergne: Verso.
4. A. Sivanandan, 2009, 'Catching History on the Wing: Conference Speech', *Race & Class* 50(3): 94–8, emphasis in original.
5. Bradley and de Noronha, *Against Borders*.
6. Arun Kundnani, 2023, *What Is Antiracism?* London: Verso.
7. 'Patients Not Passports', www.patientsnotpassports.co.uk.
8. Migrants Organise, 2021 'Cases into Causes, Causes into a Movement: How Can Individual Campaign Lead to Collective Justice and Structural Change?' Facebook, 19 March, www.facebook.com/migrantsorganise/photos/a.147786211933225/4152281074817032/?type=3%20.
9. Reeja Shrestha, 2023, 'The Justice for Omisha Campaign: Get Involved!', Migrants Organise, 25 October, www.migrantsorganise.org/the-justice-for-omisha-campaign-get-involved/.

10. SOAS Detainee Support, 2021, 'Our Politics', www.soasdetaineesupport. co.uk/our-politics/.

11. Kelly Hayes and Mariame Kaba, 2023, *Let This Radicalize You*, Chicago: Haymarket Books.

12. Maymuna Osman, 2023, 'A Victory for Our Housing Group', Migrants Organise, 9 February, www.migrantsorganise.org/a-victory-for-our-housing-group/.

13. Huck, 2022, 'Why We Blocked a Road to Stop the Rwanda Flight', 15 June, www.huckmag.com/article/why-we-blocked-a-road-to-stop-the-rwanda-flight.

14. Gracie Mae Bradley, 2023, 'On the Small Boats Bill', Gracie Mae Bradley's Newsletter, 13 March, https://inrelativeopacity.substack. com/p/on-the-small-boats-bill.

15. Ruth Wilson Gilmore, 2021, *Abolition Geography: Selected Essays and Interviews*, London: Verso.

16. Bradley and de Noronha, *Against Borders*.

17. Migrants Organise Member, 2021, 'Immigration Reporting and Why the Surveillance of Migrants Must Stop', Migrants Organise, 16 September, www.migrantsorganise.org/immigration-reporting-and-why-the-surveillance-of-migrants-must-stop/.

Chapter 6

1. Healing Justice London, 2022, 'The Power of Somatics for Collective Liberation', https://vimeo.com/manage/videos/758630267.

2. Allied Media Projects. 2020, "Healing Justice Principles & Guidelines - Allied Media Projects." August 31, 2020.

3. Ruth Wilson Gilmore, 2007, *Golden Gulag: Prisons, Surplus, Crisis, and Opposition in Globalizing California*, Berkeley: University of California Press.

4. Wilson Gilmore, *Golden Gulag*.

5. Lumos Transforms, 2023, 'The Resilience Toolkit 2', https:// lumostransforms.com/individuals-groups/toolkit-2/.

6. Rob Nixon writes about slow violence (2011) and Mbembé and Meintjes (2003) about 'gradual wounding' and 'letting die'.

7. 'Six Ways of Looking at Crip Time | Disability Studies Quarterly.' n.d. https://dsq-sds.org/index.php/dsq/article/view/5824/4684.

Chapter 8

1. Greater Manchester Tenants Union, 2022, 'Young Black Lives in the Inner City', https://tenantsunion.org.uk/news-stories/young-black-lives.html.

2. For a history of housing struggle in the UK, see Neil Gray (ed.), 2018, *Rent and Its Discontents: A Century of Housing Struggle*, London: Rowman and Littlefield.

3. UK Data Service, 2021, '2021 Census: Aggregate Data', Office for National Statistics, http://dx.doi.org/10.5257/census/aggregate-2021-1.

4. See, for example, A. Murie, 2016, *The Right to Buy: Selling off Public and Social Housing*, Bristol: Policy Press.

5. Owen Jones, 2015, 'Why Right to Buy Has Been a Definitive Disaster', *The Guardian*, 14 August, https://www.theguardian.com/commentisfree/2015/aug/14/right-to-buy-scheme-disaster-housing.

6. R. Ward, 1975, 'Residential Succession and Race Relations in Moss Side, Manchester', PhD thesis, University of Manchester.

7. E. Simon and J. Inman, 1935, *The Rebuilding of Manchester*, London: Longmans, 64.

8. Ward, 'Residential Succession and Race Relations in Moss Side'.

9. Ward, 'Residential Succession and Race Relations in Moss Side'.

10. *Moss Side News*, 1969–70, courtesy of the Ahmed Iqbal Ullah Race Archive.

11. *Black Voice*, 1969–75, courtesy of the George Padmore Institute.

12. G. Wheale, 1979, 'Citizen Participation in the Rehabilitation of Housing in Moss Side East', PhD thesis, University of Manchester.

Chapter 9

1. Erica Chenoweth, n.d., 'The Success of Nonviolent Civil Resistance', Harvard Kennedy School, www.nonviolent-conflict.org/resource/success-nonviolent-civil-resistance/; see also David Robson, 2019, 'Nonviolent Protests Are Twice as Likely to Succeed as Armed Conflicts – and Those Engaging a Threshold of 3.5% of the Population Have Never Failed to Bring About Change', BBC, 14 May.

2. A. Markandya and M. González-Eguino, 2019, 'Integrated Assessment for Identifying Climate Finance Needs for Loss and Damage: A Critical Review', in R. Mechler, L. Bouwer, T. Schinko, S. Surminski and J. Linnerooth-Bayer (eds), *Loss and Damage from Climate Change*, Cham: Springer.

3. A. L. Fanning and J. Hickel, 2023, 'Compensation for Atmospheric Appropriation', *Nature Sustainability* 6: 1077–86.

4. Jason Hickel, Dylan Sullivan and Huzaifa Zoomkawala, 2021, 'Plunder in the Post-colonial Era: Quantifying Drain from the Global South Through Unequal Exchange, 1960–2018', *New Political Economy* 26(6): 1030–47; G. K. Bhambra and J. Holmwood, 2023, 'The Trap of

"Capitalism", Racial or Otherwise', *European Journal of Sociology* 64(2): 163–72.

5.   K. Paul Harpreet, 2021, 'Towards Reparative Climate Justice: From Crises to Liberations', *Common Wealth*, April.
6.   Climate Reparations Network, https://climatereparations.uk/.
7.   Climate Accountability, 2022, 'East Africa Crude Oil Pipeline: EACOP Lifetime Emissions from Pipeline Construction and Operations, and Crude Oil Shipping, Refining, and End Use', https:// climateaccountability.org/wp-content/uploads/2022/10/CAI-EACOP-Rptlores-Oct22.pdf.

Chapter 10

1.   Refuge, n.d., 'Facts and Statistics', https://refuge.org.uk/what-is-domestic-abuse/the-facts/.
2.   Janice Haaken, 2010, *Hard Knocks: Domestic Violence and the Psychology of Storytelling*, London: Routledge.
3.   Andy Ricketts, 2015, 'George Osborne Announces Extra Funding for Domestic Violence Refuges and Armed Forces Charities in Summer Budget', *Third Sector*, 8 July, www.thirdsector.co.uk/ george-osborne-announces-extra-funding-domestic-violence-refuges-armed-forces-charities-summer-budget/policy-and-politics/article/ 1355284.
4.   Aurorand.org.uk, 2015, 'Devastating Cuts to Portsmouth Domestic Abuse Services', 9 December, www.aurorand.org.uk/devastating-cuts-to-portsmouth-domestic-abuse-services/.
5.   *Islington Gazette*, 2015, 'Holloway Prison to Close, George Osborne Announces', 25 November, www.islingtongazette.co.uk/news/local-council/21237159.holloway-prison-close-george-osborne-announces/.
6.   National Audit Office, 2020, 'Part 3: Transforming the Prison Estate', in *Improving the Prison Estate*, www.nao.org.uk/wp-content/ uploads/2020/02/Improving-the-prison-estate.pdf.
7.   Ministry of Justice, 2016, 'Prison Safety and Reform', https://assets. publishing.service.gov.uk/media/5a80aa1040f0b62302694ceb/ cm-9350-prison-safety-and-reform-_web_.pdf.